C000176266

Contents

Chapter One	From Alehouses to Zel Bars	1
Chapter Two	All Hands to the Pump: Brighton Breweries	8
Chapter Three	Dens of Iniquity: Sex, Sin and Scandal	15
Chapter Four	Wine and Spirits: Haunted Pubs	21
Chapter Five	Propping Up the Bar: Memorable Characters	26
Chapter Six	Time Out: Gay Pubs Past and Present	34
Chapter Seven	On the Wagon: The Temperance Movement	40
Chapter Eight	Pulling In the Punters	50
Chapter Nine	From Public House to Private House	62
Chapter Ten	Last Orders? Pubs in Post-War Brighton	66
Name Above the Door: How Some Pubs Got Their Names		74
Brighton's Theme Pubs		77
Index		79

All photographs courtesy of Royal Pavilion, Libraries and Museums, Brighton & Hove except where indicated.
"Brighton Boozers" logo designed by Nigel Cunningham, Royal Pavilion, Libraries and Museums.

CHAPTER ONE

From Alehouses to Zel Bars

Like many features of British life, pubs started with the Romans, who introduced tabernae – wine shops often located along roads, complete with name signs. Britons preferred (hopless) beer to wine and created their own alehouses and taverns. From the 14th century, ale was made with hops and called beer, and sold in (where else?) beer houses. Even Elizabeth I was reputed to be a regular visitor to inns. According to Jerome K Jerome's 1888 novel, *Three Men In A Boat*, the Virgin Queen *'was nuts on public houses…there's scarcely a pub of any attraction within ten miles of London that she does not seem to have looked in at, or stopped at, or slept at, some time or other'*.

The Unicorn, 1890s, corner of Queens Rd / North Street, c1892

From 1552, anyone who wished to sell ale had to obtain a licence from the Quarter or Petty Sessions; they also had to declare that they would not keep a 'disorderly house'.

By 1791, some of Brighton's most famous pubs were already established: *The Spotted Dog* (now *The Hop Poles*), *The Greyhound* (now *The Fish Bowl*), *The Cricketers*, *The Castle*, *The Dolphin*, *The Black Lion* and *The Unicorn*. Brighton's early women publicans included Mary Barnard, *Blacksmith's Arms*; Elizabeth Furner, *The Gun*; Sarah Barnard, *The Hammers*; Mary Thorpe, *Seven Stars*; and Grace Johnson at *The Spread Eagle*. Some early Brighton publicans often doubled up their professions: Joseph Davison, a landlord at *The Unicorn* and the *Sussex Arms*, was publican of the *Sussex Arms* in East Street.

The burgeoning 17th and 18th century stagecoach trade saw many inns spring up, including *The Star & Garter, The Castle, The Crown, The Blew Inn* and *The White Horse*. In 1784, the number of coach services increased dramatically, coinciding with the first visits to the town by the Prince of Wales and his entourage, which helped turn Brighton into a fashionable resort. A ferry service from Brighton to Dieppe, which started in the 1780s, and the introduction of mail coaches operating between London and Brighton, also drastically increased coach traffic. By 1820, over 60 coaches were operating between Brighton and major cities and towns. In turn, this created the separate saloon and public bars – 'outsiders' were seated outside of the coach and drank in the public bars, while 'insiders' were invited into the innkeepers' private parlours, i.e. saloons.

By 1800, Brighton – which then had only 1,200 private houses – had 41 inns and public houses. But thirty years later, the town's reputation as *'the Queen of Watering Places'* would be sped along by legislation introduced by the Duke of Wellington.

The thinking behind the 1830 Beer Shop Act was partly to reduce the public demand for gin – 'Mother's Ruin' (although publicans merely responded by opening more gin palaces); thus came the creation of the beer house, which fell outside magistrates' jurisdiction. From 2 October 1830, anyone whose name was on the rate books could open their house as a beer shop (and brew beer on the premises), without licence, for a fee of two guineas paid to the Excise office. Beer shop proprietors, unlike licensed publicans, did not have to show proof of good character or financial stability. The Act also abolished beer duty and set opening hours: 5am to 10pm, apart from Sunday service times.
100 licences were granted in the first week of October 1830 alone, but only two of the original beer houses to have opened in Brighton in first two years have survived: *Regency Tavern*, which began life as *The Gate*, and the *Druid's Head*.

In the wake of the Beer Act, pubs became more commercialised, with publicans taking a more professional approach to their trade, aware of their legal responsibilities. A legal precedent set in the Court of King's Bench 1831 added to their woes: in December 1830, a Miss Kent had been staying at a Brighton inn when 60 shillings' worth of bank notes were stolen from her room. She successfully brought an action against Shuter the landlord and the appeal judges concurred that the verdict was correct and that the keeper of an inn was *'responsible for the safety of all property'*.

In 1845, excise duty was abolished on glass, which nearly halved the price of bottles. Glass production became cheaper and beer was sold in bottles and served in glasses, instead of tankards and mugs. A commentator in *The Times* noted dryly, *'It will, no doubt, have some effect on the price of the cheaper kinds of liquor sold in bottles'*.

In 1869, beer houses came under the same licensing regulations as pubs and taverns and the 1872 Licensing Act gave magistrates powers to grant licences, fixed closing times for pubs from 11pm-6pm, and also prohibited sale of spirits to under 16s.

By the early 1890s, the number of Brighton's hotels, pubs and beer shops had reached nearly 600. But between 1900 and 1935, the number of licensed houses in Brighton dropped from 700 to 479 – a decline brought about by the First World War (which led to pub opening hours being reduced by the Defence of the Realm Act 1915), the influence of the temperance movement (see Chapter Seven: On The Wagon for more on these issues) and the economic depression of the late 1920s and early 1930s.

A product introduced by the Kruger Beer Company of New Jersey in January 1935 would also have an impact on British pubs: the first canned beer, Krueger Cream Ale, went on sale. In December 1936, a small Welsh brewer, Felinfoel, created the UK's first canned beer, Felinfoel's Pale Ale. The production of beer in cans halted during World War II but, in the post-war era, sales rocketed from 1.5 million cans sold in 1954, to 70 million by 1957. This figure increased even more rapidly when, in the 1960s, supermarkets were allowed to sell alcohol.

In April 1939, while the country was bracing itself for the inevitability of war, three members of the Brighton Health Committee embarked on a pub crawl – with the public's best interests at heart, naturally. Councillor Joseph Sherrott had claimed that many of the town's pubs were 'insanitary and unhealthy'; the Health Committee decided that the only way to find out whether the claims had any foundation was to see for themselves and so, on Thursday 13 April, councillors Briggs, Thompson and Reeves – accompanied by Chief Sanitary Inspector A H Holt – embarked on Brighton's first 'official' pub crawl, at their own expense. After visiting six pubs – a relatively modest 'crawl' – the refreshed councillors declared themselves satisfied with the cleanliness of Brighton's watering holes. The declaration of war had a curious effect on some Brightonians: in September, six men ended up in front of magistrates on drunk and disorderly charges, arising from a fracas at the *King's Arms* in George Street. While James McCue was being arrested, he swore at PC McLachlan and said, *'There's a war on. Let's have a fight now'*.

The Great Globe – a wartime 'local', Edward Street, 1965

In World War II, the pub became a social centre for bomb-torn communities, including more women customers – pubs had gone from 'gin palaces' to 'public houses' to being 'the local'. Forces and civilians alike stood elbow to elbow in the saloons and public bars; cellars, including those of *The Hanbury Arms* and *The Great Globe*, became air raid shelters. But Eileen Cooney, landlady of *The Bath Arms*, also remembered it as a tough time for publicans: *'Few people braved the blackout in winter. Sandwiches vanished with food rationing and then we had a beer shortage and could open only at limited times.'*

From Easter to November 1941 – and, again, in 1942 – Brighton was a 'Banned Area': no daytrippers or holidaymakers were allowed in the town, and even visitors coming for medical or convalescence reasons were forbidden entry.

However, the war did have one positive side-effect in Brighton: a continual decrease in the number of prosecutions for drunkenness, although the Deputy Chief Constable of Sussex, Captain Hutchinson voiced his concern in *The Brighton Herald* about a rise in the *'over-indulgence by persons engaged in national service'* and under-age drinking. In 1942, one 15-year-old girl was arrested and sent to a Salvation Army home after being found drunk in the company of 'overseas soldiers'. Others fell foul of the law after a drink or ten: in 1939, Albert Nicholls was convicted of breaking the black-out laws after displaying a light at his home at 57 Dudley Road, while Sheila Brown of Edward Street was arrested for being drunk and disorderly in King's Road. Once in the police cells, she declared that she wanted to die, and proceeded to kick the gaoler and bite the matron.

The late 20th century rise of the 'nouveau' pub in Brighton, where

The eco-friendly Earth and Stars, Windsor Street, 2005

many traditional pubs have been given trendy, youthful makeovers, spearheaded by companies including C-Side and Zelgrain, still divides opinion. The companies' detractors have accused them of 'ruining' perfectly good traditional pubs, removing all vestiges of their character and only being interested in making a fast buck.

Zelgrain was taken over in 1999 by Gavin George and Peter Bennett. Since then, their pubs have increased in number from eight to 26, including *The Mash Tun, Grand Central, The Hanbury* and *The Marlborough*, with a rapid turnover increase since then of 800 per cent. The company say they are committed to 'minimising negative environmental impact and maximizing community benefits. They were the first Brighton-based company to adopt a 'carbon neutral' policy – planting trees in Uganda to compensate for the carbon dioxide emissions eminating from their pubs, and thus reducing the impact on global warming. In this respect, the *Earth and Stars* pub is their flagship venue: everything is recycled, there are solar panels on the roof which provide heat for water and most of the drink and food served is organic.

5

C-Side was started by promoter Martin Webb and businessman Simon Kirby in 1994. The company's first pub, *The Squid and Starfish*, was a true DIY enterprise: Webb would nip down to B&Q for the materials, helped decorate the pub and worked behind the bar and even on the door. By the time the company was sold for £13.5 million in 2001, C-Side's 'empire' consisted of 28 pubs, bars and clubs, including *The Fortune of War* and *The Gloucester*. In May 2004, Webb set up a new registered charity, People's Pubs, and spent £150,000 of his own money renovating the *Robin Hood* in Norfolk Place, the UK's first 'charity pub', complete with traditional Italian pizza oven and free wireless internet. All profits – expected to be around £50,000 a year – after staff and suppliers are paid, go to worthy local causes.

Webb told *The Times*, '*I don't think people are going to come for charity. They will come because it's a good pub.*' In August 2004, he announced that the *Robin Hood* was making around £7,500 a week and People's Pubs made six donations of £1,000 each to organisations, including a women's refuge, a children's hospice, an old people's home and an HIV support group.

The hotly-contested debate about the future of Brighton's pubs, old and new, looks set to continue, wherever two or more people are gathered together – over a drink.

Charity begins at the pub, 2005

CHAPTER TWO

All Hands to the Pump: Brighton Breweries

I n the Middle Ages, ale was usually brewed in the alehouse were it was drunk. Most of it was done by women, who became known as 'brewsters'; beer was also brewed in homes and on farms.

Brighton's oldest brewery, the *Black Lion*, was established in 1545 by Flemish Protestant Deryck (originally Dirick) Carver. The original brewery building was three old tenements with dormer windows and roof made of Horsham stone. Carver was martyred for his faith at Lewes in July 1555 – burned at the stake in a beer barrel. The *Black Lion* name lasted considerably longer than its founder. One of its many owners was William Chapman, 'brewer to his majesty' and a leading member of the Brighton Hunt Committee. He died in 1823 but the brewery continued as Chapmans, under the management of Benjamin Davis, with pubs including the *Hand In Hand* and *Noah's Ark*. Brewing ceased in 1901, when the buildings were sold to the Rock Brewery, who used them for stores. Fremlin Brothers bought the premises in 1914 and used them as a bottling store until 1968, when the buildings were sold at auction and mostly demolished.

The rise of commercial breweries took off in the 17th and 18th centuries. Isaac Grover's West Street Brewery, established in 1767, was the first in Brighton to use steam power. Taken over by Vallance and Son in 1824, it became Vallance & Catt brewery. Brighton's earliest brewers also included William Chapman, Robert Hillick and James Buckle, Elizabeth Lucas, and Richard Whichols.

Smithers was founded in 1851 by Henry Smithers; his son, Edward, served as chairman of the Brighton Brewers' Society. Smithers eventually acquired the West Street Brewery, Portslade Brewery, Bedford and North Street breweries. Its Western Road premises were demolished in 1923 to make way for the Imperial Arcade.

The Black Lion Brewery, Black Lion Street, c1895

By the late 19th century, as well as boasting hundreds of pubs and beer houses, Brighton had more than 10 sizeable breweries. By the 1890s, big breweries had already begun buying up large numbers of pubs which then became 'tied houses' – i.e. the pubs could only sell the brewer's own beer. This contentious practice of 'tied houses' continues today.

Brighton's breweries included:

- Albion Brewery
- Albion Steam Brewery, 33 Chapel Street, probably absorbed into the nearby Chapel Street Brewery, 30 Chapel Street (Kirkpatrick & Co)
- Anglo-Bavarian Brewery
- Atlas Brewery, 112 London Road (William Hooker)
- Bond Street Brewery, founded in 1822 by Theophilus Pollard. He went bankrupt in 1826 and the business was taken over by John Yates – who suffered the same fate in 1838.
- Brighton Brewery – which was in Hove (actually), in Osborne Street
- Bush Brewery, sold by auction in 1826.
- Castle Brewery, 25 Castle Street (WG & S Ashby)
- Crown Brewery, Albion Hill (Thompson & Co)
- Griffin Brewery, 102 Western Road
- Gloucester Brewery, 122 Gloucester Road – in 1971, builders developing a site for the Southern Publishing Company Ltd unearthed broken stoneware beer and cider flagons bearding the trademark, 'John Dowling, Gloucester Brewery, Brighton'. Dowling opened the brewery in 1856 to make ginger beer, and began producing beer from 1864. The brewery was finally sold in 1899 by John's son, Henry.
- Queens Park Brewery, 57 Carlton Hill, run by Thomas Bird, former landlord of the Heart and Hand in Ship Street.
- Regent Street Brewery (Keeping & Bradley)

The Cannon Brewery in Russell Street was established by John Barnett in 1821. He and wife Eliza had been brewing their own beer for some time, which John would peddle around town at 3d a pint. The brewery eventually built up into a chain of some 50 pubs, including *The City of London, The Liverpool Arms, The Cranbourne Arms* and the *Montpelier Arms*. When John died in 1871, Eliza sold the business and its pubs to the brewing brothers, John and Frederick Kidd.

In August 1936, Rose Still narrowly escaped being crushed by 70 beer crates, full of empty bottles, that crashed to the pavement in Russell Street from a Cannon brewery lorry.

The brewery buildings survived until May 1969, when they were demolished as part of the Churchill Square development.

The Bristol Steam Brewery – later the Kemp Town Brewery – was started in the 1839 by coal merchant William Hallett who built most of Kemptown; it was bought by the Abbey family in 1889. Their beers included the bottled Brighton Lager Ale, which they claimed was good for the digestion. The brewery's fermenting vessels were made of rare New Zealand kauri pine, which may have given the beer its unique flavour.

Abbey's was a business blighted by several catastrophes: in March 1900, labourer John Hope choked to death on carbonic acid gas after – despite repeated warnings – climbing into a fermenting vessel to retrieve some equipment that had dropped in there. In 1907, Abbey's Eastern Road malting house was gutted by a fire which started when the kiln overheated. It destroyed six months' worth of malt.

The company was taken over by Charringtons in 1954 and the final beer was brewed and bottled in April 1964. The site was bought by Brighton College in 1967 and turned into its Maltings block. The rest of the buildings were sold in 1970 for the Seymour Square development.

Henry Abbey was once Mayor of Brighton and an alderman. His son, William, took over as chairman of the brewery, as did his eldest son, John in 1943, when it had become the Kemp Town brewery. He was also appointed High Sheriff of Sussex in 1945. After serving during World War I, John turned his attentions to collecting antiquarian books, especially those produced by private printing presses, eventually becoming England's most extensive rare book collector.

The Amber Ale/Longhurst Brewery was established by Henry Longhurst. Brighton Corporation paid £25,000 in 1901 to acquire the Preston Circus site for its tramways. Brighton Fire Station HQ (1901) and the Duke of York's cinema (1910) were subsequently built there.

The Rock Brewery – originally known as Griffiths – in 61 St James Street, started in 1809, with malthouses in Hereford Street and Warwick Street.

George Griffith, son of the original owner, was a much-loved benefactor of Brighton, whose philanthropic pomps and works included the redecoration of the Banqueting Room in Royal Pavilion. In February 1849, Griffith was found dead in the road, shot through the heart at point-blank range, about four miles from Henfield on his way back from collecting cash from Horsham. The murder weapon turned out to be one of two pistols Griffith carried with him. Robbery was believed to be the motive for the unsolved killing.

Ready to deliver: Tamplins draymen, Newhaven Street, c1936

In 1900, the Rock Brewery bought the College Brewery in Montague Place and, a year later, the Black Lion Brewery. The Portsmouth and Brighton United Breweries bought a large share of the business in 1927. By 1953, the Rock Brewery had produced its last beer and the company was wound up in 1960. The main building was demolished in 1978, and the site is now occupied by Lavender House and St Mary's Church House.

The Anchor Brewery in 57 Waterloo Street was started in the 1830s by Ebenezer Robins. Anchor beers included the 'Bottled Half and Half' – a mixture of ale and porter, a family table ale, East Indian pale ale and Brighton stout.

But perhaps the most prominent of all the Brighton brewers was Tamplins. At its peak, the company owned 200 Brighton pubs and was producing nearly 5 million gallons of beer a year. Between 1892 and 1929, it bought the Albion, Cannon, Brighton, Anchor (Robins), Smithers and West Street breweries. Tamplins itself was bought by Watney Mann in 1953 and closed in 1973.

The brewery was founded by Richard Tamplin in 1820 but, after a fire destroyed its original site at Southwick, he opened the Phoenix Brewery in 1821 between Albion Street and Southover Street. His son Henry took over on his father's death in 1849, and he was succeeded in turn by his son William in 1867. By the late 1880s, Tamplins had over 80 pubs. This number almost doubled when Charles Catt, a partner in Vallance & Catt, owner of the Ship Street Brewery since 1850, sold his 74 pubs to Tamplins in 1899 and joined their board (the brewing side of

Tamplins, Albion Street, c1935

Vallance and Catt was taken over by Henry and Percy In Willett and run as the West Street Brewery until this in turn was taken over by Smithers in 1919).

The company continued to prosper throughout the early part of the 20th century: beer sales rose from £361,013 in 1925 to £397,572 in 1927, and bottled beer sales, from 83,065 in 1925 to 120,324 in 1927.

But, by 1932, its fortunes had taken a slight, but discernible, downswing. Costs were increasing: the maintenance of horses, carriages and motors plus the company had to spend more on advertising. A number of Tamplins pubs, including *The Flying Scud, The Bath Arms* and *The Fisherman At Home* were also consistently making a loss.

After swallowing up most of its brewing competitors, Tamplins itself was bought by Watney Mann in 1953. By the time of its closure some 20 years later, when the last brew was made, it employed 450 people. The brewery was demolished in 1980 and one of Brighton's most famous names was history.

The Raven Brewery, 35 Vine Street, was set up in 1979 by pub owner, Vincent

O'Rourke; the company was producing 150 barrels a day at its peak, with most of the beer sold at the *Coachmakers Arms* in Trafalgar Street, which Raven owned. Sadly, the company fizzled out during the 1980s.

Now, only two micro-breweries exist in Brighton: the *Hand in Hand*, and the *Dark Star*.
The *Hand in Hand's* Kemptown brewery, at 33 Upper St James Street, believed to be England's smallest, was started by Bev and Brenda Robbins in December 1988 and produced its first brew in November 1989. The idea came – as many of the best ideas do – from a beery evening enjoyed at (where else?) The Great British Beer Festival in Leeds. Kemptown's three regular beers are *Kemptown Bitter, Ye Olde Trout* and *Dragons Blood*, but other brews have included *Crewsaver, Celebrated Staggering Ale* and *Staggering in the Dark*. When the Tour de France came to Brighton, Kemptown commemorated it with a special beer, *On Yer Bike*.

The Dark Star brewery, named after a Grateful Dead song, began as a micro-brewery in the cellar of the *Evening Star* in Surrey Street in 1994. Its current beers include *Over The Moon, Spiced Vice* (made with coriander), *Espresso Stout, Meltdown* (made with Chinese stem ginger) and *Natural Blonde*, made with organic malt. Its other exotic brews have included *Delhi Beli*, garlic-flavoured beer and tandoori beer – surely one of the most blatant attempts ever made by a brewer to curry favour with its customers.

CHAPTER THREE

Dens of Iniquity:
Sex, Sin and Scandal

The Castle (demolished 1948), Castle Street. Original drawing, 1818

Many of Brighton's pubs have a dark side to their history. 17th and 18th century smugglers made use of the many cellars that ran from pubs like *The Druid's Head*, *The Bush* in Arundel Road and *The Great Globe* in Edward Street to the beach. *The Sea House* – formerly *The Ship In Distress* – in Middle Street was favoured by smugglers in the late 18th century, when it as situated on a cliff edge. It was rebuilt on its new site in 1822.

In the 18th and 19th centuries, *The Coach and Horses, Kings Arms* and *The Castle Tavern* were cock-fighting centres; dog-fighting and badger-baiting were also common. Beerhouse keepers often supplied the animals.
On December 28 1795, a four guinea silver cup was contested by eight cockerels, no heavier than 4 pounds 10 oz, at half a guinea entrance fee, while on 28 December 1772, *The Castle* announced:

'a Welch Main by for a silver tancard, value eight guineas, by sixteen cocks. No cock to exceed 4lb 4oz.
Eight battles before dinner, and dinner to be ready by one o'clock'

15

By the end of the 1850s, there were known to be at least 600 prostitutes and 100 brothels in Brighton. Prostitution was rife in pubs in the Edward Street area, such as the incongruously-named *Good Intent* and *The Golden Boot*. A Miss Read kept a brothel at nearby 46 Edward Street during the 1860s and herself was arrested and fined £30 for being drunk and disorderly. Several neighbours presented a letter to The High Constable, complaining about *'the house being the resort of improper characters'* and about Read's frequent drunkenness. It was observed by a local reporter that *'several of the streets leading from Edward Street towards the Downs are crowded with brothels, where scenes of the greatest depravity are enacted'*.

Prostitutes also worked areas and pubs frequented by soldiers, such as *The George*. *The Colonnade* in New Road was also popular at theatre and music-hall closing times. Some pubs doubled up as brothels; *The Park View*, a 'gentlemen's dining club', was rumoured to offer unusual dishes on its menu. Sometimes the women came to unappetising ends: in 1794, the head of a prostitute was found in a public well near *The Sussex Tavern*.

The man believed by some crime historians to be responsible for the most notorious prostitute murders of all was once a customer at *The Cricketers*. In 1994, author Melvin Harris claimed that London journalist, former Army doctor and occult enthusiast Roslyn D'Onston was the real Jack The Ripper. According to Harris, just prior to the horrific Whitechapel murders of five women in 1888, D'Onston came to Brighton to plan the killings, and subsequently booked himself into a London hospital for a rest cure, giving his last address as 'The Cricketers Inn, Brighton'. D'Onston wrote about the Ripper murders for a number of London publications, including *The Pall Mall Gazette*. After the fifth murder, D'Onston was struck down by serious illness which incapacitated him for many years – a plausible explanation for the sudden cessation of the killings, if Harris' claims are true.

Occasionally, guests at Henekey's *New Ship Inn*, Ship Street, died in mysterious circumstances. On August 14, 1770, the Reverend James Gwynn, principal of Oxford's Brasenose College, ordered dinner, went for a walk – and was found dead, unmarked and fully-clothed, in a barley field a few days later. In 1789, Chevalier Maupeau left the pub and shot himself, leaving large amounts of gold and silver in his room.

Violence of all kinds has dogged many Brighton pubs in every century. On 28 March 1811, the High Constable put criminal John Fuller, convicted of passing off a "2d" note for £2, in the pillory outside *The King and Queen*, an event which attracted 5,000 spectators. It was Brighton's first pillorying and local shops shut early so everyone had a chance to witness the momentous event. Fuller was in the pillory from 12 to 1pm, during which time the crowd taunted him.

In April 1844, PC Huggett, whose beat included pubs *The Fox, Richmond* and *Hanover Arms*, was viciously attacked by an Eli Mockford after 'escorting' him from *The Fox*.

A Ripper haunt? The Cricketers, Black Lion Street, c1940

In February 1 1866, 'Mad' John Leigh walked into *The Jolly Fisherman* in Market Street and shot his sister-in-law, Harriet Harton, the landlady, four times. Leigh had recently been released from Petworth prison, where he had served four months after smashing up his house in a rage – he had just been turned down for a licence to run a pub in Brentford. On his release, Leigh discovered that Harriet had told his abused wife, who had been subjected to a number of violent attacks in the past, not to see him again; it was thought that Leigh also intended to kill his wife, but was apprehended before he could commit the second murder. Harriet survived long enough to identify her murderer, who was subsequently executed on April 9 at Lewes prison.

In 1844, John Lawrence, a suspected thief, was arrested in *The Great Globe* and taken to the Town Hall, where he attacked and killed Brighton Chief Constable Henry Solomon. Three years earlier, The Globe was the venue for an attempt by the police to stop voters being bribed during the local elections by keeping 18 men in the pub, with constables stationed outside to stop anyone leaving.

Marlborough landlord Tom Packham killed his wife Lucy in a drunken argument in March 1900; he was charged with murder and tried in July of that year. Lucy's father Edward Vigar testified that Packham had a long history of violence towards his wife, including trying to cut her throat and threatening her with a pistol. A policeman also testified that, while in the street outside the pub, he had heard Packham say to his wife, *'You're a lazy woman. You ought to be killed. I will kill you'.* The jury also heard from the Packhams' housekeeper, Bertha Virgo, who said that her employers were *'of very intemperate habits'.*
Despite his history of violence, Thomas Packham was convicted of manslaughter and jailed for a mere four years.
In September 1909, Lily Smallwood, a 16-year-old children's nurse, was accidentally shot dead by 6-year-old Ernest Marley, the son of her employer, Ernest senior, landlord of *The Good Intent*, while playing with one of his father's shotguns.

During the 1930s, *The Lion and Unicorn* in Sussex Street was the venue for lots of fights involving soldiers and sailors. Women customers would set about each other too, sometimes with pokers. The street was known locally as 'murder alley'.

Tommy Farr, ex British and Empire heavyweight champion, took over the *Royal Standard*, Queens Road in the 1940s, decking the walls with boxing photos. Farr lost his licence in 1945 after being convicted of assault – his behaviour was deemed to be a little below the belt when he ejected a group of drunken sailors who had refused to leave the pub.
That same year, James O'Donnell was jailed for six months for malicious wounding and assault; he had been one of a gang of six who, for months, had been going into Brighton pubs and threatening customers, often demanding money.
The genteel reputation of *The Regency* was tragically shattered in 1990 when landlady Jackie Penfold collapsed and died after football yobs wrecked the pub following England's loss against Germany in the World Cup semi-finals.

Murder most foul, Green Dragon, Sydney Street, 1987

In 1994, David 'Mad Dog' Soar murdered and robbed Thomas Connor in the toilets at *The Green Dragon* in Sydney Street, after being thrown out of *The George* in Trafalgar Street where he had been involved in an argument with Punch and Judy man, Seargeant Stone.

Some pubs were actively involved in crime-prevention. An upstairs room at *The Running Horse* in King Street was Brighton's first courthouse and, in the early 19th century, the Brighton Society for the Prosecution of Thieves held their meetings at *The White Lion* in North Street.

During both World Wars, Canadian soldiers were often involved in bar brawls which, occasionally, ended in tragedy. In June 1917, 29-year-old Theophilus McCoubrey, already the worse for wear, went for a drink at *The Flowing Tide*. After pestering two women, McCoubrey picked a fight with a one-armed Scottish soldier called Billy and his pal. The fight spilled out onto Russell Street and ended with McCoubrey dying in the Dyke Road Military Hospital. During World War II, Canadian soldiers frequented *The George* in West Street, and punch-ups were common.

In March 1944, the police vehemently opposed the renewal of *The Hervey Arms'* licence. Representing their claims, solicitor Sir Alfred Davies said, 'The scenes *outside that house night after night, week after week, and month after month are of disorder, disturbances, rowdyism and debauchery'*. Davies also said that *'persons of bad character frequented the house'* – in this case, *'women who left their children for hours outside the public house'*.

In the early 20th century, facing pressure from the increasingly powerful temperance movement, many pubs cleaned up their acts. The 1931 Royal Commission on Licensing set out to 'make the public house… a place where the public can obtain general refreshment, of whatever variety they choose, in decent, pleasant and comfortable surroundings'. Many pubs were modernised, with the introduction of better lighting, a bigger food menu – and women's toilets.

The vast majority of Brighton's pub licensees appear to be well aware of their responsibilities with regard to public safety: in 1986, the Brighton Licensing Project was set up to make pubs safer, with measures including better staff training and police liaison and, in 1999, a large number of Brighton pubs took the extraordinary step of displaying posters of known drug dealers.

However, even Brighton beach could be turned into a den of iniquity, given the right circumstances. In February 1884, it became an al fresco pub when twelve 26 gallon casks of wine and several of Burton ale were washed ashore at Black Rock after the vessel *Simla* foundered off the Isle of Wight.

The Times reported that:

'*An extraordinary scene of drunkenness followed, numbers of men and boys lying about helplessly intoxicated, many of them insensible. One boy of 15 and two others were found to be so bad that they were removed to the Sussex County Hospital and were detained, the stomach pump being brought into requisition. A man named Mockford who was found in a cave on Saturday, having apparently been lying in a state of intoxication since Friday night, has since died'*.

CHAPTER FOUR

Wine and Spirits: Haunted Pubs

Around 30 Brighton pubs are said to have more than their fair measure of spirits – and not just in the optics.

In the 19th century, a seven-foot tall figure called Old Strike A Light, complete with cloak and conical white hat, was seen at *The Rising Sun* in Pool Valley by French fishing boat captain Sivan Jervoise. Standing at the door of the closed pub – from where he and some of his crew saw strange lights emanating – Jervoise thought he heard someone striking a light with flint and steel. When the door opened, the skipper saw the imposing figure and let out a blood-curling shriek. He was brought into the pub and was sitting by the hearth, being comforted with a jug of ale, when he let out another scream, pointed and passed out. Before dying of shock the next day, the Frenchman managed to tell his story to a Father Anselm of the Order of St Bartholomew. One explanation for the apparition was that it was a hoax staged by smugglers who wanted to stop keep customers out of the pub's cellars where they kept contraband. *The Rising Sun* was demolished in 1869 and Brill's Baths built on the site – this seemed to permanently dampen the spirit, and Strike A Light never struck again.

Smuggling played a part in creating one of the *Druid's Head's* resident ghosts, rumoured to be that of a smuggler who, in 1742, was chased by customs' officials down the pub's tunnel, which ran from its cellar to the old fish market on the beach. The man is said to have fallen down the steps and died, and his ghost is responsible for bottles being moved around and glasses being smashed. In 1994, a barmaid saw a woman in a red dress standing behind another customer at the bar. But when a barman went to serve the scarlet woman, she faded away.

Like the *Druid's*, the *Royal Pavilion Tavern* has a maze of passages in its basement, which may also account for its haunted reputation. In the 1970s, some of the staff spotted a man heading upstairs to the pub's private residence. But when they chased him to the top of the stairs, they found nothing – except a locked door.

In the 1990s, *Cricketers'* landlady Sue Griffiths saw the figure of man in a cloak and wide hat. A woman customer using the toilets reported that, when the lights were off, she felt two hands stroke her forehead. *The Bath Arms* in Meeting House Lane has been visited by male figures in

More than bottles in its cellar...Druid's Head, Brighton Place, 1964

Victorian attire, and bottles and glasses have moved of their own accord. In 1966, *The Bugle Inn* was plunged into chaos by a poltergeist that played with door locks, moved furniture around, and flick the lights on and off. The ghost was nicknamed 'Charlie' by landlord Dennis Johnson.

The *Prestonville Arms* in Hamilton Road was said to have a ghost who could move heavy boxes and crates around in the cellar without making a sound.

The Harlequin in Providence Place – once a church hall – has been visited regularly by a spectral monk and a ghostly young blonde girl, while *The Pump House's* spectral occurrences are said to include strange voices, footsteps, a woman in white – and a woman in black. A lady in grey was said to frequent The Sussex in East Street, though longtime licencees of the pub, Roy and Pam Pockney said in 1974 that they had never seen her. *'I'm just waiting for the day she appears'*, said Pam, *'We'll get her to join the team. She can help with the washing-up'*.

The Stag in Upper Bedford Street has a ghost who has been named 'Albert' by the locals – the figure of a tall man wearing a white apron who used to make frequent appearances. Some of his exploits included throwing a beer barrel down the stairs, draining an entire barrel dry, turning off the taps and throwing glasses off the bar.

Early in 2001, it was reported that the management of the *Ha! Ha! Bar* in Pavilion Buildings had to call ghostbusters after experiencing strange noises and glasses being broken.

The *Eagle* pub/bakery in Gloucester Rd, was formerly the *George Beard* and, in the early 1800s, a police station stood on the site. The sounds of chains rattling have been heard and the ghost of a female jailer has been seen on the steps leading down to the cellar.

Some pubs are haunted by ghosts that have precipitated, or been caused by, more tragic events.

The ghost of Lucy Packham – in misty white form – killed by her husband Tom in 1900, is said to haunt the pub to this very day; the sounds of rattling chains have also been heard in the bar.

In 1936, Henry Metcalfe, landlord of *The Lion* in St James Street, shot and killed his wife before turning the gun on himself. One theory had it that supernatural occurrences in the pub were to blame for Metcalfe's actions.

The Franklin in Lewes Road – then known as the *Lewes Road Inn* – was almost completely destroyed on 20 September 1940 during an air raid. Amongst the dead were the landlord and landlady Ernest and Rosina Sully and their window-cleaner, John Watson. The pub was rebuilt, since when shadowy figures have been seen by staff.

In 1996, the ghost of a coach driver, complete with cloak, was reportedly seen drifting around the front door and the men's toilets of the *Battle of Waterloo* in Rock Place. He is said to be the driver of a local mayor who was murdered by a highwayman shortly after leaving the pub.

A section of the cellar at *The George* in Trafalgar Street was once used by a funeral director's nearby as an 'overflow' mortuary – hence the eerie experiences that have subsequently been reported, from gas cylinders being mysteriously turned off, to the figure of a woman giving a helping hand in the kitchen.

The cellar of *The Rock* in Rock Street also doubled up as a mortuary in the 18th century, when bodies of smugglers killed in skirmishes with Customs officials were brought from the surrounding fields and farmland. In the 1990s, a medium offered to help the pub rid itself of years of ghostly goings-on, especially the presence of an excise officer who was attacked by smugglers, and dropped down the pub's 50 foot well with a noose around his neck.

Even one of the new 'theme' pubs, the *Australian Walkabout* on West Street – once the New Regent – has not been immune from paranormal punters. A man in chef's clothing – nicknamed 'Claude' – has been seen in the bathroom and on the staircase. Claude may, in this life, have been a former employee, Mr Webster, who hanged himself there in 1903.

Haunted by a tragic past – Bedford Tavern, Western Street, 1982

The *Bedford Tavern's* cellar is allegedly haunted by the ghost of a pregnant woman who died there after being given a bed by the landlady, where she gave birth to a stillborn baby. By the morning, the woman was also dead. Child-like fingerprints seen on panes of glass at the *Star and Garter* (now *Dr Brighton's*) may stem from the death of a 19th century child in the cellar. More than a century ago, the landlord performed illegal abortions and sometimes the children of the women recovering from the procedure would wait in the cellar for their mothers to return. One little boy was playing in the cellar when he smashed his head on a barrel and died soon afterwards.

A ghost at *The Regency* is also said to be that of a child – a small, disabled girl who worked for cobblers and lived in a room over the shop. One night, she woke up and, thinking she could smell gas, jumped out of a window in a panic and died. In the 1990s, Jim Liddle, landlord of the *Park View* in Preston Drove, spoke about the odd events he had experienced at the pub, including gas bottles by the stairs being turned off. An American woman, whose grandfather had once been the *Park View's* licensee, came to visit the pub and, after doing some research,

discovered that, during the 1920s, a little girl had fallen down the stairs – the very

Shall we dance? The Bat & Ball, Ditchling Road, 1986

space where the gas bottles were later stored – and died. Jim Liddle was unperturbed by the youthful spirit, saying that '*The ghost only plays childish pranks, nothing really horrible happens*'.

Some former landladies have apparently found it hard to leave their pubs. In 1991, a female figure in a white nightdress danced through the bar at the *Bat & Ball* – it transpired that an extrovert former landlady used to do just that. Emily Edlin, former licensee of *The Regency*, is said to be a permanent fixture at the pub. *The Mash Tun* – formerly *The Volunteer* – has experienced unexplained footsteps, bulbs shooting out of lamps and clothing scattered about rooms. The events have been blamed on the spirit of Martha Boxell, who ran the pub during the First World War.

One pub that has never reported any ghostly goings-on – though you might well have expected it to – is *The Hanbury Arms*. The pub was formerly the Sassoon family mausoleum, built in 1892 for wealthy merchant Sir Albert Abdullah Sassoon, who was buried there four years later. His son, Sir Philip Sassoon, sold the building to the Kemp Town Brewery in 1933 and his ancestors' coffins were removed for reburial in London.

CHAPTER FIVE

Propping Up the Bar: Memorable Characters

Photo courtesy of Marion Devoy

Thomas and Sarah Burtenshaw, 1867

Brighton's boozers have enjoyed their fair share of larger-than-life personalities – on both sides of the bar.

In February 1908, conjoined twins Violet and Daisy, the daughters of barmaid Kate Skinner, were adopted by Mary Hilton, midwife and landlady of the *Queen's Arms* in George Street and, later, the *Evening Star* in Surrey Street. While at the *Queen's Arms*, Mrs Hilton sold postcards of the 'Brighton United Twins' in the bar for twopence. Sensing greater fortunes could be made, she pushed her adopted daughters into showbusiness and they left to forge a successful career in America in 1924. They formed their own vaudeville show, The Hilton Sisters Revue and toured regularly. The sisters also appeared in two films, Tod Browning's 1932 classic *Freaks* and *Chained For Life* (1951), which boasted the somewhat lurid tagline, '*Siamese Twins Playthings Of Desire*'.

The Hiltons topped the bill at the Brighton Hippodrome on several occasions and were fondly remembered in the town. Former theatre attendant Albert Dunk recalled seeing them walking around: '*A crowd would gather to watch them and invite autographs, and they would always oblige, always smiling and without any sense of embarrassment. They were such charming girls*'.

The Hilton Twins retired from showbiz in the 1950s and fell into poverty and obscurity. They were working on a supermarket checkout at the time of their deaths in 1969, discovered in their apartment by their employer after they failed to show up for work.

The Hiltons did not follow their adoptive mother into the pub trade, but many Brighton publicans have carried on the family tradition.

Young widow Emily Edlin took over the license of the *Regency Tavern* in 1893, and in doing so, laid the foundations of the Edlins firm whose pubs would include *The Great Globe*, the *King and Queen, Abinger House* and the *Regent Tavern*. Emily died in 1933, at the age of 91; her last public appearance was when she laid the foundation stone for the new *King and Queen*, where Edlins would also have their company offices.

As well as being a director of Edlins, Tubby Edlin was also a comedy actor, appearing in melodramas and pantomimes, also appeared in concert parties and toured with his own company of entertainers. He also starred in the 1930 film, *Alf's Button*, alongside Nervo and Knox, the Crazy Gang stars.

In the early 20th century, various members of the Burtenshaws, one of Brighton's longest established families, ran a number of pubs, including the *Good Intent*, and *The Mechanics*. Thomas and Sarah Burtenshaw ran the *Welcome Brothers* on the seafront arches; they later moved to *The Jolly Brewer* in Ditchling Road and eventually bought Tongdean Farm – now the Tongdean estate.

The Burtenshaws sold the *Welcome Brothers* to pleasure boat Captain Fred Collins, one of the town's most famous characters.

Upon his death in August 1912, aged nearly 80, the *Brighton Herald* lamented: '*It has robbed Brighton of an institution. It has deprived the Brighton beach of an integral part of itself. It has deprived pleasure seekers all over the world of an old friend. He was as much of an institution of Brighton as the Chain Pier used to be*'.

For over fifty years, Collins ran his bunting-clad Skylark pleasure boats from Brighton's beach opposite the bottom of West Street, giving rise to the familiar phrase, '*Any more for the Skylark?*'. One of his most famous passengers was Charles Dickens, a regular visitor to the town for short breaks, who wrote to a friend in 1867, '*The sea was rather choppy and his chatter to the trippers was very witty and amusing*'.

Collins held annual benefits for the Royal Sussex Hospital, and was eventually made one of its governors. His son, Fred junior, helped his father and took photographs of holidaymakers; he also ran a photographic studio in Kings Road arches.

Fred Collins' funeral brought Brighton to a standstill: his widow received over 750 telegrams and messages of condolence, and the mourners included the Deputy Mayor and representatives from Smithers & Son and the Brighton & County Beer Retailers' Association. However, amongst all the public outpourings

of grief and expansive obituaries, no-one bothered to mention an episode that occurred during his time as a pub landlord – an episode that could have left the good captain high and dry.

On August 1, 1877 Collins and his son, Frederick Poste, were charged with the manslaughter of boat builder George Winder, at their pub, the *Welcome Brothers*. On the evening of 21 July, Winder became embroiled in an argument about being wrong-changed with young Fred Collins, who was working behind the bar. Winder went behind the bar, and a fight started between him and the two Collins, ending up with Winder being thrown over the bar by Fred senior, according to a witness, 'with great force'. Other evidence also stated that they had never seen Winder the worse for drink. Winder died the next day from his head injuries, and Collins and son were arrested, granted bail, and committed to stand trial for murder in March 1878. Two fellow publicans, Leonard Burton from the *Lamb and Flag*, and James Boyles of the *William IV*, both in Church Street, paid the sureties.

At the trial, Lord Chief Justice Cockburn's summing up clearly directed the jury to acquit both defendants, stating that Captain Collins' actions were, in the circumstances, completely justified and made much of the medical evidence that Winder had a thin skull and being slung across a counter did not necessarily cause his death: 'If there was any reasonable doubt with regard to this matter, Collins was entitled to the benefit of it'. The case against Fred junior was dropped due to lack of evidence that he had struck Winder during the fight. Without leaving the court, the jury returned a verdict of 'not guilty'; Judge Cockburn said of Collins that the case should be a warning to him: 'I have no doubt hehad been very much provoked but in future he must take care and not let his passions get the better of him'.

The ferocious gales that battered Brighton in February 1965 uncovered a reminder of Captain Collins: the storms stripped away six foot of shingle to reveal the rusty iron chains that once shackled the Skylark boats and the stone steps down which thousands of day trippers had tottered to enjoy a few hours at sea. A more permanent memorial was the naming of an 846 bus, 'Captain Frederick Collins'.

Edith and Henry Hazelgrove ran the *Pedestrian Arms* in Foundry Street for over 50 years, from 1922. Edith was born there in 1896 and worked behind the bar from the age of 12, when its opening hours were 5am to 11pm; she also used to play piano in the saloon bar. The pub was in her family for 90 years: Edith's mother, Alice Pettett, took it over from 1915, after the death of her husband Thomas, and then handed it over to new son-in-law to Henry in 1922. Born in Bread Street, Henry's aunt, Polly Bourne, once owned most of Brighton's beach huts. He and Edith were childhood sweethearts and married in St Peter's in 1921. The Hazlegroves' pub became known as 'the postman's pub'. *'It was a tiny place, and I didn't want to be a publican'*, Henry said, *'but when I came out of the army, jobs were scarce.'* The fisherman's son founded the Brighton Deep Sea Angling Festival and the Publicans' Association Fishing Club.

Lily Holloway was born in 1892, in the *Three Jolly Butchers* in North Road, the pub run by her parents. Her father died in 1900 and her mother married William Jefferies, who became the new landlord. More than 70 years later, Lily remembered vividly the role of *The Butchers* and the area's other pubs: *'In those days, there was the Burtons' blacksmith's at 61 North Road. Children used to watch them shoeing the horses. There was the Regent Foundry Iron Works at 63, Mr Woolgar's bakery at 55, the Norfolk Castle Inn at 54, the Moulder's Arms and the Founders Arms. All the postmen used our pub, so did the players from the Eden Theatre opposite which later became the Grand. Monday nights in the pub were for the laundry girls, Wednesday was the grocers' night out. Fridays were for the soldiers from Preston Barracks and the drill hall in Gloucester Road and on Saturdays country folk crowded into Brighton to shop. It's still the best pub in the district.'*

An era came to an end in February 2004, with the death of Brighton's last old-style landlady, Winnie Sexton, publican of *The Cricketers* for 19 years; she spent a total of 50 years in the pub trade. *'She was one of the kindest souls you could ever meet'*, said her friend Eva Petulengro, *'She always remembered people and what they drank, even if she hadn't seen them for years'*. When flower-loving Winnie (even her

Watering hole to the stars: The Volunteer, Church Street, c1976

frocks were floral) retired in 1992, her customers collected £3,500 to buy her a round-the-world ticket.

Other colourful Brighton publicans have included Ray Fury, the former European light-heavyweight wrestling champion who became landlord of the *Admiral Napier* in 1982 and 92-year-old Albert Martin who, in 1945, was declared the country's oldest publican. Mr Martin, landlord of the *Park View*, had then been running the pub for 38 years.
Eddie Scannell, landlord of *The Marlborough* for many years, entered the World Cocktail Shaking Competition in the 60s, with a red cocktail called Flame. *'It had a base of Tia Maria liqueur to which was added Lillet and Grenadine with ice'*, he explained. *'Just one of these, and you began to feel happy'*.

Pubs near theatres and music-halls, including the *Colonnade, The Volunteer, The Wheatsheaf* and *William IV* have always been favourite watering holes for a host of showbiz stars, Elizabeth Taylor to John Gielgud, Trevor Howard to Peter Finch. Writer Jeffrey Bernard, (first unwell, now deceased) and an aficionado of England's watering holes, once declared that, *'Generally the pubs of Brighton are not up to much, but The Volunteer is a decent sort of place'*.
In 1974, Horace Hunter, publican of the *Queensbury Arms*, recalled how *'Lord Olivier came in here with dark glasses and very dull clothes and an old pair of carpet*

slippers and he put on such a wonderful act – pretending to be an old man – that I thought no-one but him could act like that. And, of course, that's who it was. He drank a half bottle of champagne. He just sat in a corner next to a lorry driver and no-one knew who he was. There's real democracy for you'.

Brighton resident, the writer – and imbiber extraordinaire – Lord Robin Maugham was a regular face at the *Colonnade*. Another Brighton resident, the infamous TV panelist Gilbert Harding, was a devoted customer at *The Sussex*. In 1960, when publicans George and Edna Taylor moved from *The Sussex* to the *Waggon & Horses*, Harding sat outside the pub in his car on their

Harry Cowley, hero of the poor, 1949

first day, determined to be their first customer. A different type of hero was a regular face at the *Free Butt*: Harry Cowley, the chimney sweep who tirelessly campaigned for the poor and homeless of Brighton.

In 1651, a Brighton pub entertained a guest who, in unusual circumstances, was fleeing for his life. Six weeks after the battle of Worcester, King Charles II was being pursued by Cromwell's forces. On Tuesday 14th October, he rode 60 miles from the house of Thomas Symonds in Hambledon, Hampshire to Brighton, together with supporters Lord Wilmot and George Gunter, to the *George Inn*. Gunter had scrutinised the pub for safety and decided it was a safe place for his charge to spend the night. The King took the best room, and enjoyed wine and dinner. The *George's* landlord recognised his royal guest but, fortunately for Charles, he was not a Roundhead loyalist. The exact location of the *George Inn* continues to be debated by local historians. Some claim the pub was the *George Inn* at 1 West Street, while others argue that it was the *George Inn* that was subsequently renamed the *King's Head*, at 9 West Street, and a third candidate was identified as *The George* in Middle Street. On 15th October, six weeks after the battle of Worcester, the *George Inn's* trio of guests left for Shoreham harbour, where they boarded a boat called the *Surprise* and landed at Fécamp in France the next day.

Another loyal Royalist was a resident at the *Albany Tavern* which stood on the corner of Duke's Lane: John Townsend was a famous Bow Street runner who guarded the Prince Regent when he was staying at the Royal Pavilion.

In the early 20th century, 'Blind Harry' Elwes was a Brighton street entertainer, an accordionist who worked the seafront. After finishing at his regular pitch, he would repair to the *New Pier Tavern* in Preston Street, where he would impress customers with his piano repertoire, watched over by the landlady, the improbably-named Mrs Overall. It's rumoured she may have left the pub trade and gone on to become the cleaner at a family-run antiques business in Manchesterford…

Ellen 'Bubbles' Ashworth was a big frog in *The Pond*. This flamboyant lesbian lived in 24 Frederick Gardens for 25 years, many of them with her partner Zena Dell. In her later years, Bubbles was a regular fixture during the lunchtime sessions at *The Pond,* the pub just across the street from her home.
Her favourite tipples were Holsten Pils and gin and water; she always ensured that not a drop of Mother's Ruin went to waste by putting more water into her empty gin glass and swilling it down. According to friends, Bubbles had an astonishing repertoire of ribald drinking songs and poems. She died at her home in 1993, in her favourite chair, waiting to be escorted to *The Pond*.

Not all of Brighton's pub regulars were homo sapiens. Bill Smith, landlord at the *Waggon & Horses* in the 1970s, remembered the days when *'It was like a farmyard behind the pub. It smelled just like the countryside. At one time there were horses, a goat, chickens, dogs, cats, a sheep and some ducks – all living happily together right in the centre of Brighton'.*
In the 1930s, Alfred Appleton, landlord of the *Prince Albert*, advertised the feats of his 'Trickster Dog', Peggy, in the local press. The spaniel would entertain customers by laying the table to order – complete with cutlery et al in its correct place – and fetching her master any drink that he requested.
In 1975, a horse was invited into the bar of the *Stable Inn* and given a glass of beer: *'He drank it in one gulp',* said landlord Roy Pockney. *'It must be thirsty work, being a horse'.* During the 1980s, Ernest Ruffer, a regular at the *Windsor Tavern* in Church Street, always brought his pet tortoise James to join him for a drink.

Many groups, from knitters to Dungeons and Dragons fans, organic gardeners to gay real ale enthusiasts, meet regularly in their favourite Brighton pubs. But one group which has long since supped its last is still fondly remembered by pub historians.

The Ancient Order of Froth Blowers was set up in the 1920s to raise money for various charities. Their regalia included playing cards and ceramic tankards with the motto 'Moderation' printed on the inside. Their membership literature declared asked potential members 'Do you gollop your beer with zest?' and bore the greeting, 'Ale Fellow, Well Met!'

The Brighton and Hove Order of Froth Blowers was founded by a Bert Temple and presided over by chairman

Entertainer 'Blind' Harry Elwes, c1905

'Monsoon' H Thorpe Oliver; they held their inaugural dinner at the Old Ship Assembly Rooms on Thursday 24 February, 1927, where members sang the Froth Blowers' anthem, 'The More We Are Together', countless times. Further musical entertainment was provided by none other than Tubby Edlin. 'The Grand Hurricane' David Cain declared that the organisation 'must not be on any pretence whatever be regarded as an excuse for boozing – for charity and conviviality, yes, but drunkenness, never'. And he spouted forth a motto as memorable as it is difficult to say after an evening at the pub:

'Lubrication in moderation'.

CHAPTER SIX

Time Out:
Gay Pubs Past and Present

Photo courtesy of Brighton OurStory

Kay Morley and friends enjoy a drink on the steps of Pigott's, c1955

In 1951, Brighton MP William Teeling told the town's Hotels and Restaurants Association: *'There is no reason why we should not make ourselves a very gay town from now on'.*

But anyone visiting the right pubs would have known it already was.

From the 1930s, Pigott's bar at the *St James Tavern*, 16 Madeira Place was popular with gay visitors and locals alike. Colin Spencer remembered Pigott's as *'full and very noisy...the women were mainly middle-aged, in severe but formal clothes. Could these women really be disciples of Sappho? But undeniably this bar was their life. They sang to the playing of the piano, romantic ballads of the 30s when they had been young girls first falling in love'.* Pigott's regular, Sheila, started going there in 1950 when she was 20, and in Brighton Ourstory Project's *Daring Hearts*, remembered *'This little lady [Dolly] used to play at the piano with her jangling bracelets, cigarette hanging out*

of her mouth…it was
terribly small. It was quite
tatty, all really dark
brown. It was just
ordinary working-class'.

Another early gay
favourite was the *New*
Pier Tavern. Here,
according to local
writer John
Montgomery, there
could be found 'a
sprinkling of red-
coated, pink-faced
guardsmen and sailors

'The G' — a welcome for gays in East Street, 1974

from Portsmouth'. The *Thurlow Arms* in Edward Street, near the old market, was a
good place for picking up equally pink-faced barrow boys.

In the 50s and 60s, a favourite haunt was the *Albemarle* near the Palace Pier,
where customers would sip drinks *'in a palm court full of potted plants and other*
rare flowers, and could stay upstairs for six and seven a night including breakfast'.
Another post-war gay-friendly venue was the upstairs bar at *The Greyhound* (now
the *Fish Bowl*) – known to regulars as *'The G'* – run by Edie behind the bar and
May on piano, who also took messages for customers across the bar, tucking the
notes behind bottles. Other popular pubs were the *Golden Fleece* in Market Street
and the *Spotted Dog* (now the *Hop Poles*). According to John Montgomery, these
pubs were so discreet that *'visiting mums and dads who stray into them by accident,*
usually think them rather dull'.

Women with short hair and sensible shoes frequented the seafront pubs, the
Fortune of War and the *Belvedere* which, as recalled by Eddie in *Daring Hearts*, was
presided over by a large blonde lady called Queenie who 'was as tough as teak'.
The *Belvedere* was the setting for writer Colin Spencer's first play, *The Ballad Of*
The False Barman. He remembered the pub as *'the essence of all low dives since the*
beginning of time…there were always a few weary gay boys on the game, looking thin
and hopeless…with names that struck me again like poetry – Banana Lil, Big Molly,
Lazy Sadie'.

Others whiled away their evenings at the *Quadrant's* upstairs bar in Air Street, where pianist Charlie Neate's saucy singalongs on Saturday nights were often interrupted by raids from 'Lily Law'.

On 1 Feb 1972, Sussex GLF members met n the upstairs bar of usually gay-friendly *Greyhound*. However, on this occasion, the manager announced *'This is not a homosexual bar!'*, forbade them from distributing their leaflets, and told the barman not to serve them any more drinks. The group's regular venues were the upstairs bar at the *Stamford Arms* (now *Circus Circus*), then *Markwell's Bar* on the seafront, and finally the *Marlborough*. All three pubs held regular GLF discos.

In 1973, the police descended on Brighton's pubs during their investigation into the murder of 63-year-old London accountant Thomas Wilson, known to have been a frequent visitor to the town; one theory was that Mr Wilson met his murderer at a Brighton pub and then took him back to his London home. Interestingly, the police team was headed by Det Chief Roy Ranson, who was to return to Sussex the following year – to lead the hunt for the fugitive murder suspect Lord Lucan.

Until the establishment of Brighton's LGBT police liaison group, mistrust of the police throughout the community remained widespread for decades. A 1990 survey carried out by Brighton Area Action Against Section 28 in pubs revealed that over half those questioned would not go to the police if they suffered a homophobic attack and some of those who had were then subjected to verbal abuse by officers. Furthermore, during the investigation into the murder of barman Peter Halls that year, many pub-goers were asked intrusive and irrelevant personal questions which would have had no bearing whatsoever on the case and were horrified when it was later disclosed that this information would be kept on police computers for up to ten years.

The derelict *St James Tavern*, which dated back to 1810 when it was built as a private house, with beams made from old ship's timbers, was bought by Geoff and Josie Waters in 1976 and re-opened as the *Bulldog* in May 1978 (its earlier name was sold to the pub opposite); it is now Brighton's longest-established, openly gay pub. By the mid 80s, the pub had become so popular its downstairs bar was described by Brighton gay author and journalist Peter Burton as resembling *'a railway carriage at rush-hour'*. Famous faces who have boarded the 'carriage' include Dora Bryan and June 'Dot Cotton' Brown.

Throughout the 1970s and 80s, gay-friendly pubs came and went, and included the *Princess Victoria* in Upper North Street, the *Caxton Arms*, North Gardens and the back bar at the *Iron Duke*. The *Oriental* in Montpelier Road became a popular drag venue; decorated in Far Eastern style, it was once listed in the Guinness Book of Records for its small bar, measuring just 9ft x 3ft.

A spot for sporty ladies… The Dorset Arms, North Road, 1983

The *Cricketers* enjoyed a popularity with gays which, according to Peter Burton, was 'probably encouraged by the camp landlady' – Winnie Sexton.

Camp interiors were undoubtedly a factor in the *Regency Tavern* becoming a favourite venue. It's also the venue for Lesbian Link socials, now going strong for 20 years.

The pub known as the 'old' *Heart In Hand* at 65 Ship Street was given a camp nickname by its gay regulars – one which replaced the 'heart' with another body part… From the mid-70s, the *New Heart in Hand* at 80 East Street featured drag acts. In a 1982 edition of *Gay News*, regulars were much amused by a misprint for the pub which declared, 'Gays we come'.

The *Hanbury Arms* was a venue for weekly 'dyke discos' in the late 70s and early 80s, and in the early 80s, Brighton Lesbian Group held socials on Sundays and Wednesdays at *The Dorset Arms*. Regulars were told by the landlady Irene Shields that they were the 'Ladies Sports Club'. Irene was no stranger to sporty ladies: she had previously run the *Quadrant*, the *Belvedere* and the *Fortune Of War*.

The Rockingham, Bedford Road, Sillwood Street, 1986

By July 1981, the *Spotted Dog* was now 'under new management' and Ted Pritchard, one of its regulars, was told by the new licensee 'I don't want your kind in here'. *Gay News* contacted the landlord, ex-policeman Norman Riches, who told the magazine, *'There has been a complete change of policy and we no longer welcome gays at The Spotted Dog'*.

In 1984, the *Rockingham Inn* (now the *Lion and Lobster*) was Brighton's most popular gay pub, with three bars. Opposite was *The Caves* drinking club, very popular with lesbians, which stayed open an hour later than the pubs.

The *Queen's Arms* at 8 George Street – home a hundred years ago to the conjoined twins, Daisy and Violet Hilton – has been at the heart of Kemp Town's gay scene for decades, and now offers entertainment seven nights a week. The *Black Horse* in Church Street, then a popular drag pub, was dubbed 'The Pink Pony' and, for years, the sign above the door bore both names. St Bartholomew's church hall in Providence Place underwent a conversion of a non-religious kind and is now *Harlequin's*, which features drag and other cabaret entertainment. By 1990, the *Aquarium Inn* in Steine Street was offering strippers, cabaret, drag and *'the spunkiest barmen on the coast in the friendliest pub in town.'* The *Queen's Head* at 4 Steine Street became another addition to the gay pub scene in 1990, even though *Gay Times* writer Bill Short thought licensees Chris and John had gone *'a bit over the top with the Laura Ashley and Victoriana'*. Others thought the pub had gone over the top yet again when, following the death of Freddie Mercury, its name-sign sported a portrait of the late *Queen* singer.

In the face of – until recently – local and national government resistance to recognising the rights of gay organisations to public funding, gay pubs have been integral in funding Brighton's modern LGBT community, raising thousands of pounds for Pride, AIDS charities, local switchboards and groups. The town now boasts a host of out and proud venues, including the *Marlborough, Dr Brighton's, Marine Tavern, Bedford Tavern, Brighton Tavern, The Stage,* the *White Horse* and the *Candy Bar,* the town's first full-time lesbian venue.

One of the most recent additions to the LGBT pub scene is *The Jury's Out* on Edward Street, opposite – where else? – the law courts. When new owner Alan Evans took it over in September 2004, it was, he says, 'extremely run down and had a terrible reputation'. Conscious of this – and mindful of the increase in homophobic attacks around the St James Street areas in recent years, Evans installed CCTV and hired security. Now, both gay and straight people in the neighbourhood use the pub; Alan adopted *'a zero tolerance approach to any forms of abuse, discrimination or intimidating behaviour…several women have commented it on being the only pub they would visit on their own'*.

Customers in all these pubs today might do well to pause, raise a glass and say 'cheers' to the queers whose brave, bar-room forays in the last century ensured that William Teeling's vision of Brighton as a 'gay town' was no drunken dream.

CHAPTER SEVEN

On the Wagon:
The Temperance Movement

Karl Marx claimed that religion was 'the opium of the people'. In the 21st century, sport, celebrity gossip and reality TV could equally qualify as latter-day opiates. But, in the mid-19th century, a cross-section of Victorian society was in no doubt about what kept the masses enslaved: alcohol.

By the mid-1870s, the average annual consumption of spirits per man, woman and child was 1.5 gallons, and the yearly consumption of beer per head from 1895-1900 was 31.2 gallons. Beer was much stronger in Victorian and Edwardian times than modern ales, and sometimes extra salt was added to increase drinkers' thirst. This, coupled with the image of 'gin palaces' and beer houses as breeding grounds for all manner of social ills, helped fuel the temperance movement. It brought together a coalition including Catholics, Methodists, Quakers, the Salvation Army, Non-Conformists, working men and women – and the wealthy worried. Initially, spirits – particularly gin – were the temperance targets, but it soon embraced all alcohol. Some factions advocated moderation, while others favoured total abstention, with hardliners demanding a ban on the sale and consumption of alcohol. In response to the criticisms, some publicans did start selling beverages, including ginger-beer, lemonade and soda water. In 1904, the Brewers' Society (later the British Beer & Pub Association) was founded, with the objective 'to protect and promote the interests of the Brewing Trade'. In their first year, the Society's main concerns were not the rise of the temperance movement, but the continuation of war taxes on beer and spirits, three years after the end of the Boer War conflict during which they were imposed.

Victorian middle-class philanthropists, including Joseph Rowntree, were the most concerned about the affects of drinking on the working classes.
George Sims, author of *How The Poor Live* (1889), and a temperance supporter, wrote:
'Drink is the curse of these communities... The gin-palaces flourish in the slums, and fortunes are made out of men and women who seldom know where tomorrow's meal is coming from. Drink is sustenance to those people; drink gives them the Dutch courage

Sons of Temperance Convalescent Home, Tower Road, c1904

necessary to go on living; drink dulls their senses and reduces them to the level of the brutes they must be to live in such places. The gin-palace is heaven to them compared to the hell of their pestilent homes'.

This was certainly true in the poorer areas of Brighton, such as Carlton Hill, Albion Hill and Edward Street – pubs like the *Vulcan* were at the heart of poverty-afflicted community, housed in buildings with no sinks or toilets, and eventually condemned as unfit for habitation.

And Philip, Viscount Snowden – Ramsay MacDonald's Chancellor of the Exchequer – observed that, *'temperance alone would not touch the root causes of low wages and poverty. Universal temperance would undoubtedly bring incalculable benefits and blessings, but so long as the social system is based upon exploitation, the mass of the people will remain comparatively poor'.*

Britain's first teetotal pledge was signed in 1832 by eight men in Preston, and the first teetotallers' society formed in 1835. But it was not until 1868 that the Brighton branch of Sons of Temperance was set up, consisting of 12 members. Its aims were *'to provide through regular contributions, mutual assistance in times of need and to encourage thrift by provision of Sickness Benefits, Life Assurance and Endowments amongst Total Abstainers'.* They produced booklets, with titles such as *'The Bottle Explains'* and banners that read *'Wine Is A Mocker'.*

The branch's youth section, the Cadets of Temperance, was formed in 1882. Like the Band of Hope, its aim was to teach children from an early age about the virtues of abstinence.

Another 18th century movement that eschewed the temptations of alcohol was the Cokelers, founded on the principles of the faith-healing evangelist James Bridges. The Cokelers did not listen to secular music or read secular books, play games, smoke or drink alcohol. However, this didn't stop them being one of the main brewers active in the Sussex cider-making industry. In the 1870s, the Brighton branch of the Sussex Cokelers used to meet at the Mission Chapel in Conway Street, Hove.

The subject of many sermons by Brighton's Victorian 'Beach Preacher', W H Shoosmith, was temperance. However, the manic beach preacher himself was no abstainer – after taking a collection at the end of his sermons, he usually spent the takings in the nearest pub, either the seafront *Norfolk Shades* or the Southover Street hostelries including *The Fox*, the *Dover Castle* and the *Hanover Arms* near his home.

Advocates like Shoosmith may have been preaching to the converted on many occasions. Antique dealer Thomas Crane had signed the pledge in late 1899 but fell off the wagon four months later when his nephew was wounded in the Boer War. Crane smashed a window at the Sussex Hotel but, after apologising for his actions and assuring the magistrate that he would *'be a teetotaler now'*, was spared a jail sentence.

In the late 19th and early 20th century, many leading figures in The Liberal Party were closely associated with the National Temperance Foundation, and The Licensing Act 1872 was introduced by Gladstone's Home Secretary Henry Bruce in an attempt to tackle widespread drunkenness. The Bill sought to limit opening hours, reduce the number of pubs and control brewers' profits. However, its provisions were watered down in response to widespread opposition from breweries, publicans and working-class drinkers. The 1872 Licensing Act displeased both sides: the Temperance advocates thought it was too lenient, while victuallers regarded it as too excessive. It certainly wasn't a vote-winner – the Liberal government lost the election two years later.

In 1900, under the Inebriates Act 1898, Brighton Council established Brentry House, a residential home for male and female alcoholics. However, the national trend told a different story. By the end of the 19th century, about one tenth of Britain's adults were total abstainers.

But this didn't stop the next Liberal Party, both in opposition and government, from continuing their attempts to bring temperance to the country through lobbying and legislation.

In February 1903, Margaret MacDonald – Ramsay MacDonald's wife – served on the National Union of Women Workers' Joint Committee on the Employment of Barmaids, which sent a resolution to London's licensing magistrates to 'consider the advisability of recommending that the employment of women in public bars shall be discontinued'. The official reasons behind the resolution were the long hours worked by barmaids in austere conditions – but, undoubtedly, the fact that they were said to 'suffer from the confinement in a close atmosphere with the constant smell of intoxicating liquors' was no small factor.

Mrs MacDonald asserted that 'the committee are strongly opposed to any action which would involve the dismissal of a single barmaid' but instead recommended 'that the licensing magistrates should accompany the renewal of licenses with the condition that no new barmaids should be engaged'.

The debate rumbled on for many months, filling the letters pages of national and local newspapers. In *The Times*, Gertrude King of the Society for Promoting the Employment of Women, asked what alternative work the ex-barmaids were supposed to find and feared that 'they will probably be driven to seek the life and excitement they love by more dangerous ways'. Another correspondent, Frances Balfour, questioned the motives behind the original resolution, pointing out that 'when a movement is set on foot in favour of restrictive measures, the public is generally told at the onset that the proposed restrictions are for the benefit of the persons restricted'.

But the pressure continued to mount and culminated in the tabling of the 1906 Employment of Barmaids Bill, which proposed the phasing out of barmaids, on the basis that 'the disproportionate number of barmaids ends in drunkenness, immorality, misery and frequently suicide'. Britain's 27,000 barmaids were, apparently, solely responsible for most of the country's social ills.

Opponents, including the Women's Trade and Labour Council, rallied against the law – 'Is any working women's trade ideal from the standard of a leisured class?', asked its Secretary, Eva Gore-Booth. The WTLC established the Barmaids' Political Defence League, which held debating meetings up and down the country, and asked for donations to support the working women who, in a most unlikely scenario, 'find themselves plunged suddenly into a political conflict of the most cruel and vital kind'.

Ultimately, the Barmaids' Bill failed to become law, but the issue reared its head again when the Liberal government tabled the 1908 Licensing Bill which, amongst other things, attempted to reduce licensed premises by a third close pubs on Sunday – and, under Clause 20, would have abolished the employment of barmaids.

This time, the opposition to the measures spread wider than women's organisations: the National Freedom Defence League came to Brighton and held an open air meeting at the bottom of Elm Grove. One speaker, Martin Judge, maintained that the new law would not prevent drunkenness and that it was merely 'nonconformist fanaticism aiming at Sabbatarianism and prohibition'.

The biggest protest against the Bill was held in London's Hyde Park on 27 September – in an era without mass media communication, an estimated 500,000 people assembled. The brewing trade laid on 130 extra trains to bring supporters – many of them from the south coast to join in. A contingent of about 1,300 people went from Brighton, including representatives from Tamplins, Abbey & Sons, Smithers & Sons, The Rock Brewery, Kidd and Hotblack, Robins & Sons, The West Street Brewery, the Beer Retailers' Association, the Licensed Victuallers' Association – and a good number of barmaids.

The outbreak of World War I gave the Liberals another chance to go into battle against the demon drink. In 1915, David Lloyd George blamed alcohol for adversely affecting war workers:

'We are fighting Germany, Austria and drink; and as far as I can see the greatest of these three deadly foes is drink, doing us more damage in the war than all the German submarines put together'.

The King evidently agreed with him: in a letter to the Chancellor, it was reported that George V concurred 'It is without doubt largely due to drink that we are unable to secure the output of war material indispensable to meet the requirement of our Army in the field', adding that 'the King will be prepared to set the example by giving up all alcoholic liquor himself'. A Royal nod was as good as a wink, and measures introduced in October under the Defence of the Realm Act (DORA) reduced pub opening hours to just five and a half – 12.00 noon to 2.30 pm and 6.30 to 9.30 pm – led to the quality of beer weakening and raised taxes on alcohol: by 1918, a bottle of whisky cost £1, five times what had cost before the outbreak of

A show of temperate strength at The Dome, c1915

war. Britain's beer consumption dropped from 89 million gallons in 1914 to 37 million by 1918. In addition, a No Treating Order decreed that people could not buy alcoholic drinks for others.

In Brighton, the spirit of Temperance was as strong locally as it was nationally. In March 1915, the PSA (Pleasant Sunday Afternoon) Temperance Committee held its annual sermon at the London Road Congregational Church, Ann Street, with guest speaker Rev. John Binney supporting greater curbs on wartime drinking. In 1917, the Carlton Hill Mission celebrated its 28th anniversary with a sermon by missionary Mr J J Jones and a speech by the Mayor Alderman Herbert Carden, who congratulated Jones on his Temperance work in the Carlton Hill area – 'If there is any district in the town needing such work, that is the district'.

Another clergyman, Rev. Lewis Court of the Bristol Road United Methodist Church, had a more immediate problem: his church was within a stone's throw of the Kemp Town Brewery and he had observed 'load after load of "ruined grain" of malt that has been converted into beer' and condemned from the pulpit 'the wicked waste of foodstuffs going on in the manufacture of intoxicating drink'.

Meanwhile, another Brighton resident, Maria Thomas, was aiding the war effort in her own particular way: in April 1917, she was sentenced to one month's hard labour for supplying wounded soldiers with bottles of stout at her home in Jubilee Street. Thomas admitted the charges, saying 'I did not think I was doing any harm'. Major Dingle from the Pavilion Hospital testified that alcohol was the worst thing for the wounded men and considered the offence to be 'serious' – a view the bench concurred with.

Always adding grist to the temperance mill has been the curiously high number of deaths in Brighton linked to alcohol – in one way or another. A few examples are:

- In April 1901, George Willard was found lying on his back with his head bleeding outside the *Swan Inn*, where he had spent most of the evening drinking. Willard died later in hospital and at his inquest a fellow lodger, bricklayer Thomas Bollan said: *'since the death of his wife, deceased has drunk very heavily'.*

- In October 1902, Robert Brooks, 38, 14 Beaconsfield Road, a former licensed victualler, died of *'liver disease and chronic alcoholism. At his inquest held at the Stanford Arms, Preston Road, his sister Annie said he 'was of very intemperate habits'.*

- Russell Watson, second brewer at the Black Lion brewery, shot himself in the company's office in October 1904. His body was found by the cleaner. No suicide note was found, and no-one had any official explanation for Watson's state of mind, although it emerged that he had recently been given a notice of redundancy, as part of the brewery's general cost-cutting.

- Edward Dexter, a lodger of *Robin Hood Beer House*, 22 Tichborne Street, choked on his own vomit in February 1905, while 'under the influence of alcohol'. The landlord, Henry May, said the *'deceased had been drinking freely during the past few days…had drank heavily of spirits for a week and had had nothing to eat. I did not supply him with spirits – he obtained them from outside.'*

- Former actor turned singing teacher Lancelot Dechamps Holt, 30, collapsed and died of 'heart failure due to chronic alcoholism at his apartment at 67 Grand Parade. Holt had been told by his doctor to come to Brighton for a rest and was sharing a bed-sitting room with retired banker Charles Galloway, whom he had known for several years. Galloway was excused from attending his friend's inquest by a doctor's note that said he was suffering 'from nervous exhaustion'.

- In May 1908, John Dawson, of 28 Upper Rock Gardens, a former licensed victualler, was found dead by his wife; he had strangled himself with his dressing gown cord attached to the curtain rail of his bed. His wife Laura said he *'had suffered from depression for some time past.'*

- Louis Snelling, a foreman brush maker died at Brighton Workhouse Infirmary in October 1911, from *'uraemic coma following liver and kidney disease aggravated by chronic alcoholism'*.

- Nurse Helen Wilson, 45, of 38 Trafalgar Street, died in January 1913, of *'heart failure caused by bronchitis accelerated by chronic alcoholism'*.

- 74-year-old Elizabeth Austin Wickens, 'a woman of intemperate habits', died at Workhouse infirmary in January 1914. Although her landlord Thomas Painter said he had never seen her drunk, Dr Arthur Duckett said Wickens' liver *'was greatly enlarged, about half as big again as it should be'*.

- In March 1918, Sarah Wright, wife of the landlord of the *King's Arms*, 56 George Street died in her sleep of alcoholic poisoning. Her husband Charlie said she *'was of intemperate habits'*.

- Florence Robbins, 42, died in 4 Arundel Terrace in 1922. For 15 years, she had been companion/housekeeper to Henry Ellis, who said she had suffered from jaundice and liver trouble. *'Lately, she had given way to intemperate habits... she was very obstinate...has been wasting away'*.

- Thomas Barnes, landlord of the *Sussex Arms* in Gardner Street, for 35 years, was found washed up on Hove beach in February 1926. His wife could not explain his death and an inquest decided it was suicide.

- Two months later, Ernest Silvester, 50, landlord of the *Bath Arms*, 3 Meeting House Lane, shot himself in his bedroom. Silvester had suffered from consumption for years, which made him depressed, and had threatened to shoot himself on a number of occasions. His niece Hetty Whittle, said: *'When my uncle did not drink anything, his health would be fairly good but when he did, the haemorrhage [of lungs] would set in.'*

By 1935, the number of pubs in Brighton had dropped by almost a third, from 700 in 1900 to 479. The Chief Constable, Captain W Hutchinson, was able to report that, though there had been an increase in incidents of drunkenness in the town, a large number were down to visitors and 'vagrants'. However, he added that *'it was unfortunate for the town that they had had several people who had not been satisfied with getting drunk once, but had been drunk on a number of occasions.*

One male was charged eight times, another five times and three others four times'. (In amusing contrast, official figures for the year 1949 showed that only one case of drunkenness occurred in Hove – this was 'a non-resident, a young girl who was persuaded to go on to a yacht and there saw some colours in bottles which she had not seen before. She was found safely asleep in the arms of Bacchus on the Sea Front at Hove'.)

In October 1935, several prominent members of the Labour Party, including lifelong teetotaler George Lansbury MP, pleaded the cause at a meeting at the Dome. Lord Arnold – ignoring the Liberals' long association with anti-alcohol policies – claimed that only Labour could provide Temperance reform. Joseph Jones, President of the Miners' Federation, asked: 'If drink is so efficacious, if it is so beneficial, why is it that alcohol is a prohibited article for the miner to take underground?', and castigated Brighton 'for being too respectable to vote Labour'.

Months before the beginning of World War II, in January 1939, no less a figure than A W Hillman, the Mayor of Hove, was extolling the virtues of pubs. Addressing the annual banquet of the Brighton and County Licensees' Society at the Royal Pavilion, he said: 'In my opinion, the facilities offered and the comfort provided today by the brewers in our boroughs and the way in which they have provided decent houses and accommodation for the public have done much to prevent excessive drinking'.
By the time World War II began, the national Temperance movement had three million members and, echoing the mood of the previous war, the National Temperance Federation issued the manifesto, 'Alcohol – A Foe To Britain':
'We therefore proclaim that it is the duty of every good citizen to confront drink, the enemy of the country, with the example of his own self-discipline and determination to abstain while the war lasts. It is equally the duty of the Government to see that Britain's strength is not wasted nor her cause endangered by the lure of drink'.

Brewers fought back with an advertising campaign, advocating beer's positive properties as nutritionally beneficial and a digestive aid. An article in the Brewer's Journal said, 'On all counts, therefore, as a war time drink "Beer Is Best", and the nation must see to it that it has a plentiful supply'. And Quentin Hogg MP countered 'Beer is the innocent pleasure of many millions, especially to those who bear the brunt today'.

In 1994, the Venerable F Smythe, the Archdeacon of Lewes, appeared to support this view when he pleaded for the breaking down of any social barrier between the Church and pubs. Speaking to Deanery churchwardens at Holy Trinity Church, he said, 'There is the England of the Church and the England of the public house. Each is suspicious of the other. It is ridiculous to suppose there should be no refreshment houses, and only people of no vision imagine the pub is all wrong or not respectable. It is a pity our climate prevents our having the continental café, but we should work for something on these lines'.

Interestingly, the Archdeacon's comments came within months of the opening of the *Norfolk LA Pub* in Grand Parade, which claimed to be the county's only non-alcoholic pub. The Norfolk offered drink, including milk shakes and fruit juices, food and entertainment from 11am to 11pm; it wouldn't even sell low-alcohol beer sold. Its owners, Pubs Unlimited, said 'What we are saying is: You don't need alcohol to have fun'.

In the 21st century, official membership of the Temperance movement has dwindled into the hundreds and, with new laws in the offing that will allow licensed premises to stay open for up to 24 hours, the Archbishop's dream of continental bar culture is drawing ever near. However, charities and support groups which deal with the effects of modern-day alcohol abuse share many of the same concerns that temperance advocates have voiced – with alarming statistics that eerily echo those from 150 years ago. According to Alcohol Concern, an estimated 920,000 children are currently living in a home where one or both parents misuse alcohol, with 6.2 per cent of adults having grown up in a family where one or both of their parents drank excessively. Another figure shows that 60-70 per cent of men who assault their partners do so while under the influence of alcohol.

CHAPTER EIGHT

Pulling In the Punters

Once upon a time, the sale of alcoholic beverages in Brighton was a simple, straightforward affair: in 1749, residents were able to go to the Block House – the 16th century circular coastal defence that stood on the cliff between Ship Street and Black Lion Street – where *'Mary Saunders, Widow, sells fine genuine French Brandy, at nine shillings per gallon'*.

Since then, of course, licensed premises of all kinds – whether they be alehouses, inns, taverns, beer houses, public houses or bars – have, in response to social and economic changes, devised myriad methods to keep punters coming through their doors. With some pubs, this has meant a radical change of image, involving redecoration, entertainments and facilities aimed at particular age groups. Others, however, have survived by resisting a cosmetic makeover and sticking to their strengths, such as real ale and traditional décor and pastimes.

As Colin Burtenshaw, chair of Brighton's Licensed Victuallers' Association has said: *'You have to cater for customers in your area – the success of your pub depends on knowing what they want'*. And George Forster, landlord of the now long-gone *City of Hereford* observed: *'There are a thousand and one things that go to make a local, and it's not the place, it's the things that go on in it.'*

In the 21st century, this means 'segmentation' – the process by which pub companies decide which category, or segment, their respective licensed premises fall into, depending on their distinctive customers and attributes.

So – is your favourite pub 'wet led' or 'dry led'?
Is it a 'Basic Local' – or a bit more than that?
Here's how it works:

BASIC LOCAL – community pubs, regular drinkers, little food, televised sport, few women, 'wet led' – *I Go Inn; Montreal Arms, Prince of Wales, Cobbler's Thumb, Leconsfield, The Stag*

MID MARKET LOCAL – 'traditional' pub a la *Corrie/EastEnders*, some food, quizzes, darts, pool. – *Waggon and Horses, Lord Nelson, Cobden, Duke of Wellington, Bat and Ball, Heart and Hand*

UPMARKET LOCAL – quality food, more women customers – *Basketmakers, Bath Arms, Druid's Head*

I Go Inn, Rock Street, 2004

YOUNG LOCAL – customers aged 18-30 from local area, modern décor/feel, pool, music and video screens, games, etc. Draught lagers are the most popular drink. – *Park View Tavern, Roundhill*

CITY LOCAL – city/town centres, basic pub food/snacks, aimed at local workers and shoppers, with residents in evening – *Office, Market Inn, Full Moon*

CITY DRY LED – central location, lots of food, may have function rooms or restaurant areas – *Sussex, Ha Ha, Pond, Dorset*

CHAMELEON – central location, daytime serving workers and shoppers, evening young people with loud music – *Victory, Coach House, Black Lion*

CIRCUIT – Young people, loud music, possibly dress code and door staff. Lager and spirits most popular, little food. – *Constant Service, Western Front, Squid and Starfish*

PREMIUM DINING – Food-led, restaurant quality, adult-oriented. – *Dover Castle, Greys, Hop Poles*

VALUE DINING – good value food attractive and welcoming to families – *Black Lion (Patcham), Battle of Trafalgar, Martha Gunn*

VENUE – wet-led pubs that offer something different e.g. live music, entertainment or internet facilities, or serves as a meeting point for specific groups – *Geese Have Gone Over The Water, Albert, Free Butt, Open House, Hare And Hounds, Marlborough, Pressure Point*

WELCOME INN

The idea of pubs providing more than a pint is nothing new, of course. As far back as Chaucer's time, inns provided food, accommodation and storage facilities for travellers. After the 1663 Turnpike Act, more roads were paved and Britain's coaching business took off, which in turn led to coaching inns opening along main routes; these provided food and drink, and also fresh horses. Visitors to the *Stag Inn* in Upper Bedford Street could buy the freshest food possible on Sunday mornings when local fishermen would bring their catch in and lay it for sale on the public bar.

Brighton's coaching inns included the *Star & Garter* (now *Dr Brighton's*), the *White Horse Inn*, from where coaches ran to London's Cheapside and the *Spread Eagle* (now the *Sussex Arms*), terminus for routes from London, Guildford and Chichester. *The Crown*, in Grafton Street, was opened in the 1830s by wine and spirit merchant William Marchant and was the stopping point for coaches running between Brighton and Rottingdean. The inn had four bars for its different types of customers: aristocracy; celebrities; 'respectable' visitors; and day trippers.

Eventually, these and other inns started to provide entertainments for guests. In 1785, the *Star & Garter* announced the arrival of the Irish Giants:
'The most surprising Gigantic Twin Brothers are just arrived in Brighthelmston and to be seen at the Star & Garter on the Cliffe, every day. These truly amazing phenomena are indisputably the most astonishing productions of the human species ever beheld since the days of Goliath. These modern Colossuses are but 24 years of age and very near eight feet high. Admittance: Ladies and Gentlemen, 1s; Servants, 6d.'

In 1807, boxing champions John Gully and Tom Cribb sparred outside the *King and Queen* before a large crowd of spectators that included the then Prince of Wales and some of his brothers. In 1808, the *Coach and Horses* held an exhibition of *'a Great Curiosity Of A Male Child, only two years and five months old, such as was never brought before the public, in this or any other country, and is allowed by the Faculty to be one of the greatest wonders ever seen'.*
What made the child so wondrous, alas, isn't on record.

A number of central Brighton pubs offered bear-baiting, dog-fighting and, in particular, cock-fighting, a popular attraction at the *Kings Arms* and the *Coach and Horses*. This pub was also the site of one of Brighton's most famous pub meals: the Billy Goat dinner, held in 1851. A goat was kept in the stables opposite and often allowed to wander freely. At that time, an order existed which decreed that all stray dogs could be shot on sight by the Beadle. Unfortunately for the goat, Beadle Billy Catlin was extremely short-sighted and, after seeing what he believed was a loose dog at the bottom of Bond Street, shot the animal. The goat's body was then taken to the *Coach and Horses*, roasted and eaten by grateful customers.

On the first day that the 1830 Beer Act came into force, the *Brighton Herald* observed that *'Many of the landlords of the new beershops gave away beef and beer on the occasion, and in some instances bands of music enlivened the street from temporary orchestras'*. The 1830s saw the rise of the so-called 'gin palaces', with their common design features of high ceilings and large mirrors – and no seats, so as to accommodate more customers. Bars were also introduced – as were barmaids. Pubs became more commercialised, with landlords taking a more professionalised approach to their trade, and their premises became venues for political meetings, markets, concerts and even coroners' inquests. Some publicans branched out by opening 'singing saloons', where admission was gained by buying a bronze or copper disc, which was then exchanged for food and drink.

By the late 19th century, many larger pubs had turned their spare rooms into music halls – or 'song and supper rooms'. The first was Canterbury Hall 'tavern and music rooms', which opened at 87 Church Street in July 1860. This was a natural progression from the 'free and easy' – amateur sing-songs in 'singing saloons', where Saturday evenings saw husbands and wives visit pubs together for an evening of musical and other entertainment.

Pre-20th century, pub recreations played an important role in working-class life, hosting horticultural shows, bowling, glee clubs and friendly society meetings. Victorian pubs also organised outings; formed Christmas clubs; held flower shows, sports contests and musical events. Single men often frequented the pubs to have their meals and peruse the newspapers. In the Edwardian era, pubs affiliated with football teams, sometimes renting land to clubs.

The Hanbury, St George's Road, 1974. From burial place to Bombay Bar

FIXTURES AND FITTINGS

Pub décor styles came in and out of favour, from the Greek and Roman styles, via Gothic and Italianate, to Art Nouveau. Victorian pubs favoured cherubs, urns, sunflowers and lilies, glazed tiles, mosaic floors, marble, brass, engraved windows and ornamental bars. By the 1890s, more pubs had installed seats and tables, and most had separate public and saloon bars. Many, such as the *Liverpool Arms* and the *Norfolk Arms*, also had designated Smoking Rooms, while others, including the *Montepelier Inn*, had Bagatelle Rooms.

In the early 20th century, especially in the 1920s and 30s, pub interiors were becoming increasingly flamboyant, reflecting the prevailing influence of the the cocktails-and-jazz era and 'Olde English' décor.

The *Bath Arms* boasted a grotto, complete with artificial waterfall, plants, moss-covered rocks, seats made of tree stumps and electric lights which looked like 'a fairy palace in miniature'. In 1922, the *Thatched House* in Black Lion Street became the first Brighton pub to have a beer garden, situated in the narrow passage between its back door and Little Market Street. Now, any pub in Brighton with the merest hint of an outside area has transformed it into another attraction for punters. The *Open House* in Springfield Road, given the Zel treatment in 2000, has one of the largest outdoor capacities in Brighton, with 40 tables, a fountain, mosaic and water feature. Other pubs to capitalize on their outdoor spaces are

the *Setting Sun*, the *Sidewinder*, The *Hop Poles*, the *Battle of Trafalgar*, The *Windmill*,

The Hampton, The Crescent and, of course, the beachfront *Fortunes Of War.*

In 1924, Edlins renovated *The Gloucester* into *'an artist's ideal of what a public house should be. The saloon bar might have served as a boudoir for Mrs Fitzherbert. The walls are paneled in brown walnut, while the mouldings edging the panels, the detail carvings and the classic motives characteristic of the style are in sober gold....the glasses and tumblers come well into the decorative scheme...the deep padded seats...there is a special ladies' bar...and a large room provided for children. Even the off-licence bar is designed on harmonious Georgian lines.'*

Another Edlins pub, the *King and Queen* has its 'Tudor' look created in 1931; its saloon bar was a replica of a Tudor dining hall, and the pub also had a Tudor courtyard with fountain and pond. The *Brighton Herald* hailed it as *'something more than a handsome, spacious building, wherein people can eat, drink and be merry in perfect comfort. It is a gorgeous flight of architectural imagination'.*

In 1953, Kemp Town Brewery acquired the *Bombay Bar*, the annexe of *The Hanbury Arms* (and the former Sassoon family mausoleum), and adorned it with murals of elephants and dancing girls, red upholstery and arabesque fittings. Edlins paid homage to Brighton's Regency history when, in 1956, they built Abinger House, on the site of the Abinger family mansion on King's Road. In its efforts to create the 'first Regency reproduction pub in England', the company consulted the Regency Society and the Borough Surveyor. The building cost £125,000, and took eight years of planning, as Edlins were keen to get the reproduction just right and scrapped many of their original plans.

Flanagans also drew on a bygone age for its relaunch of the *Seven Stars* in 1970, opting for 'authentic' Edwardian cuisine and atmosphere, with marble-topped tables, sawdust on the floor and barmaids and waitresses in Edwardian costume. The walls were festooned with adverts for haircuts and shaving, and black pudding, pies and faggots costing 3d and 6d. The menu featured jellied eels, fish and chips in paper, cockles and mussels, and apple pie and custard, and entertainment was provided by 26-stone pianist Fingers Calder and his nine-inch long moustache.

The *Regency Tavern* has become rightly famous for its rather camp interior decoration twin lion statues, velvet banquettes, oil paintings, gilt-framed mirrors – and especially the mirrored tiles and glitterball in the gent's toilets.

Other pubs went in for less flamboyant improvements: in 1974, the *Cuthbert's* beer garden, featuring a lawn, fish pond, terrace and beer barrels of geraniums, won first prize in a Courage competition. In the same year, the *City of York's* landlord, Joe O'Connor, resisted the urge to go 'modern': *'We decided that most of*

Geoff and Chris, longtime landlords of the Regency, Russell Square, 2005

the customers were aged 30-50 so we didn't put in tubular lights or a loud juke box. We made it comfortable with a touch of modern Tudor.'

For others, even the most modest of improvements could prove problematic – in 1970, new red blinds were fitted in the windows of the *Cricketers*, an act which incurred the wrath of Brighton Council's Planning Committee, which claimed that planning permission was required.

No permission was needed, however, for the hundreds of chamber pots which hung from the ceilings of the both *The Pond* and the *Green Dragon* (now *The Office*).

PLEASURE AND LEISURE

In the post-World War II era, many of Brighton's old pubs were lost to economic, leisure and urban changes. Those that survived increasingly had to offer diverse attractions, novelties and entertainments to keep the punters coming, rather than just the promise of a decent pint. Eddie Scannell, a longtime landlord at the *Marlborough* observed in 1985, *'The days when a landlord could just open his doors and expect customers to flock in are long gone. Now you have to fight for them. It is not just a drink they are after – they want to be entertained.'*

Many pubs offered live music: in 1974, you could visit *Martha Gunn's* to hear *'Ivor and Geoff entertain…they play their guitars and sing – not too noisily and not too quietly, providing live entertainment which television and radio cannot offer'.* The pub was also home to Brihota, the Brighton & Hove taxi drivers' football team. The *Richmond* (now *Pressure Point*) became one of the most popular venues for fledgling bands and the famous alike, from the Manic Street Preachers to John Lee Hooker, The Levellers (who started there) and Ronnie Scott. In 1992, arts groups and punters alike launched a passionate campaign to save the pub, after Charringtons announced they wanted to get rid of live music to *'bring the pub up-market'.* The campaign succeeded but victory was rather soured when the brewery forgot to renew its public entertainments licence and bands couldn't play at the pub for months.

Other pub entertainment included cabaret and drag shows at gay-friendly pubs, including the *Oriental* and the *Black Horse*, and 'upstairs theatre' at the *Marlborough* and the *Nightingale* (now *Grand Central*).

Other landlords opted for non-musical entertainments to keep their customers amused. During the 1970s, the walls of the *Full Moon* were covered in foreign currency and its bar covered by over 3,000 old coins, including farthings, plus framed old receipts and bills. In 1984, landlady Anita Duke, formerly of Astley's pipe shop in London, tried to turn the pub into a pipe museum, featuring a 150-year-old smoker's cabinet.

The Black Horse, Church Street, 1976: life was a drag

In 1982, *Prinny's* wine bar opened upstairs at the *King and Queen*, featuring a Beers of the World club (with members' T-shirts and ties), 30s cocktails, antique furniture and a food menu featuring *Prinny's Pie*, made according to a 16th century recipe.

The *Kensington* offered its customers no less than 250 different liqueurs from around the world, including everything from Polish spirit (which probably tasted more like spirit polish) to Japanese green tea liqueur. In 1985, the pub tried its hand at being an 'authentic' German beer keller, called the Brighton Holsten.

But perhaps Minden Haley, landlord of the *Montpelier* Inn, offered the most basic attraction to customers; in 1985, he declared that he had the most attractive barmaids in town: 'It is a fetish – no, an obsession – of mine to make sure that all the girls I take on as bar staff are real ravers'.

PUB GRUB

In the 1983 film, *The Ploughman's Lunch*, Frank Finlay and Jonathan Pryce tuck into some 'traditional fare' – the pub meal which gave the film its name. While they're eating, Finlay – a TV commercial director – explains to Pryce that the 'traditional' food they are eating, in fact, was created by a television advertising campaign in the 1960s, aimed at getting more people to eat in pubs – *'a completely successful fabrication of the past'*.

Fact seemed to bear out this fiction as, in the second half of the 20th century, publicans put as much effort into offering a decent food menu as pulling a decent pint. Now, more than 80 per cent of pubs sell food; 1.1 billion pub meals are served a year, compared with 0.7 billion restaurant meals. However, this may change: in 2004, a Government white paper contained proposals to ban smoking in all pubs where food – apart from bar snacks – is served. These proposals have led the British Beer and Pub Association to voice their concern that *'a smoking ban based on food seems designed to drive pubs back to the days when they were drinking dens'*.

In 1967, the *Vasso* became Britain's first pub where parents could take children for an ice cream or soft drink while they enjoyed something a bit stronger. The following year, the *King and Queen* enjoyed a relaunch by landlord Ken Cook, who opened up the courtyard and started serving barbecues, aiming at student population: 'I aim to offer them facilities of the sort they want, such as the music and barbecue. They are an important section of society.'

In 1969, the *Pickwick Bar* opened its *Pickwick Grill*, the *Barnaby Rudge* bar and grill, and the *Dickens Restaurant and Bar*, which welcomed families and offered a menu feauturing rump steaks with jacket spuds or chips, children's half portions, connoisseur coffees and real ale.

In the 1970s, the range of pub food available included everything from fresh crab sandwiches at the *Aquarium* to *Deryck Carver's*, no-pun-intended carvery lunches. The *Albermarle Beer Keller's* grill room offered ploughman's lunches, steak and kidney pie, scampi and plaice, steak and chips, Cornish pasties and sausages, and favourite 70s starters, avocado, melon, soup and prawn cocktail. The *Volunteer* (now the *Mash Tun*) had its *Fish Tank Bar*, *'specialising in fresh local fish'*, with lobster, sole and bouillabaisse. The *Cranbourne Arms* (now the *Western Front*) had an upstairs restaurant which specialised in business lunches and evening meals which, by the mid-80s, included Thai and Indian menus.

In the early 80s, the *Full Moon* – which had undergone yet another decorative revamp, featuring prints of 19th century coaches and collections of old cigarette cards – offered a typical menu of pasta, pizzas, rump steak, lasagne, moussaka, chilli con carne, chicken and chips, scampi, steak and kidney pie and jacket potatoes: 'a trendy snack food'. At the *Sea House's Crow's Nest* restaurant, you could munch on quiche and chips for £1.60, or instead sample one of the *Bulldog's* 24 different types of jacket potato fillings.

THEMES AND COLOUR SCHEMES

As the 20th century drew to a close, Brighton's pubs were undergoing another revolution, with the rise of 'superpubs' and an increasing number have all traditional traces removed and replaced with interiors and entertainment geared towards the town's increasingly younger population. These changes had their detractors, including Mike Morton-George from CAMRA, who said '*What is a particular shame is when pubs have been renovated and the whole look is changed so that it looks like a fast food restaurant.*'

In 1996, the Zelgrain group hoisted its flag to the mast by turning the *Volunteer* into the *Mash Tun*, offering a laid-back, under-30s atmosphere and a cosmopolitan menu to match, featuring Jamaican, Thai, North African and Cajun food. Zel also took over the *Cranbourne Arms* and turned it into the *Western Front*. In 1969, the owners, Watney-Tamplins, had given the pub a major refurbishment in an effort to keep its doors open, including removing its three small bars and replacing them with one, aiming at the lunchtime trade, including offering food and morning coffee.

Also in the 90s, the *Prince Albert*, which hadn't even had so much as a lick of paint for 47 years, was given a £100,000 facelift and the *Royal Pavilion Tavern* re-launched itself in 1991 with the opening of its *Shades* café/bar and restaurant. Its one major concession to a bygone age was the installation of the long bar that ran the length of the pub, previously used at Victoria Station during WWII.

Some landlords faced objections when they tried to spruce up their premises. In 1988, residents objected when the *Rockingham* became the *Lion and Lobster*, and its exterior was painted bright pink because, according to landlady Norma Friend, *'Before, drinkers were passing us by. It just looked like an ordinary house'*.

During the 90s, Denis Murdock, landlord of the *Sudeley Arms*, was told by council officials to take down the pub's illuminated plastic Guinness sign *'because it spoiled the character of the conservation area'*; the publicans at *Mrs Fitzherbert's* were told to remove a fake bull's backside sticking out of its exterior walls as, according to council enforcement officer Linda Rogers, *'It's backside is big, ugly and not even a good shape'*; and *The Fish Bowl* (formerly the *Greyhound*) was ordered by the planning department to removing an 8ft sign showing a goldfish in a bowl, as it was also *'out of character with the conservation area'*.

Unfortunately, no-one has yet objected – on the grounds of good taste – to the giant portrait of the late, great John Peel that now adorns the west wall of the *Prince Albert*, the pub which the DJ visited in 2003 to listen to some local bands. The picture has proved popular with foreign tourists who have been flocking to have their picture taken under it, but the man himself might be wincing in his grave at the work which owes a great deal to the curiously 'Identikit'-style portraits produced by tourist-fleecing 'artists' in Leicester Square.

Other pubs changed what they offered inside their walls, not outside.

In 1993, the *Norfolk LA pub*, which claimed to be Britain's only non-alcoholic pub, opened for business, offering food and entertainment from 11am to 11pm, and drinks including milk shakes and fruit juices; not even low-alcohol beer was sold. Owners Pubs Unlimited said, *'What we are saying is: You don't need alcohol to have fun'*. In 1996, the *Whitehawk Inn* was converted into a training centre for the unemployed, serving only soft drinks and beverages.

As far back as the early 80s, the *Pump House* advertised that it welcomed women customers on their own. Its dark panelling was stripped back and hot and cold meals were available. Claudia Baker of Vintage Inns said: *'We have designed the décor here to appeal to women, It's very light and airy.'*

However, their efforts seemed to be in vain: in 1992, the *Argus* published a survey which showed that most pub customers were still mostly men. *Pump House* landlord John Cullen said, *'Some pubs have facilities which may put women off, such as poor toilets'*.

In September 2001, the *Eagle Inn* (formerly the *George Beard*) opened a bakery on its premises, producing bread for its sister outlets, including a Greene King IPA-flavoured loaf. *The George* in Trafalgar Street – not oblivious to Brighton's reputation as the vegetarian capital of Britain – became the first fully-fledged vegetarian pub. Its success was heralded when it was named Vegetarian Pub of the Year in the 2002 Pub Food Awards. Appropriately enough, Brighton & Hove Organic Gardening Group now hold monthly socials there.

Other pubs were happy to resist making radical alterations to their image and facilities. One example is the *Great Eastern*, whose primary attraction is its lack of modern attractions: the pub is quiet and traditional, and offers a selection of 40 single malt whiskies and shelves of books for customers to enjoy perusing over their drink.

Meanwhile, Brighton's pubs continue to offer up entertainment as diverse as its clientele: open mike nights, Northern soul nights, Mexican nights, Irish nights, quiz nights, heavy metal nights, 60s nights, 70s nights, 80s nights – though no-one's yet tried to hold silent nights.

CHAPTER NINE

From Public House
to Private House

Brighton is, and always has been, the 'Queen of Watering Places', with a pub or bar to suit all tastes – in alcohol, entertainment and decoration. The numbers of licensed premises ranged from 479 in 1860, rising to a peak of around 700 in 1900, 495 in 1930, to the current figure of around 300.

Brighton's pubs and beer houses tended to be in the central retail and transport areas, especially around North Laine, but also in the poorest areas of concentrated slum housing. For instance, in 1891, Carlton Hill alone had the *Carlton Arms; George IV; Sack of Shavings; Alma Tavern; Devonshire Arms; Queen's Park Tap; Rising Sun; Morning Star; Italian Arms; John Bull; Foresters' Arms; Carlton Tavern;* and *Star Tavern.*

From 1848 to 1930, Tamplins had a pub at 135 Sussex Street called, at various times, the *Royal Yacht Anchor,* the *Royal Yacht Inn* and *The Yacht and Anchor.* Competition was stiff: this pub-dense street also had the *Little Yacht, Claremont Tavern, Lion and Unicorn, Crown and Sceptre,* the *Miller's Arms, London Arms, Highbury Barn* and *Red Lion.*

Many of the town's watering holes are now lost in the mists of time, wiped out by urban regeneration, commercial pressures and demographic changes. However, even though many of the buildings have disappeared completely, a remarkable number have survived into the 21st century.
Perhaps your current home, or favourite boutique or sandwich shop, was once a favourite 'local'…

QUEEN'S ROAD

In 1891, Queen's Road had 15 hotels and pubs – and four temperance hotels. The pubs included the *Mitre Tavern* (65), the *White Eagle* (9), *Windsor House* (25), *Alexandra* (54-56), *Crown* (63), and *Victoria Shades* (95a).

The *Terminus Hotel and Tavern Wine and Spirit Stores* were at 74, owned by George Payne. In the 1850s, he pledged that all his establishments refreshments would be 'of first-class quality' and the offered customers '*every convenience and comfort appertaining to a first-class establishment, consisting of a coffee-room, club-room, smoking-room, waiting room, private sitting-rooms, etc. Beds warranted well aired*', Only two of Queen's Road's pubs have survived: the *Royal Standard* (59) and *Queen's Head* (68-70).

SURREY STREET

If this tiny road leading to Brighton station seems to have more than its fair share of pubs nowadays, just imagine what it looked like in 1891 when, as well as the still-surviving *Evening Star* (55), the *Railway Bell* (26) and the *Railway Inn* (29, now *Grand Central*), it also boasted the *Surrey Street Globe* (11), the *Terminus Shades* (31), the *Flowing Stream* (33), the *Rising Sun* (37), and the *Comet* (41).

TRAFALGAR STREET

RAILWAY GUARD, 40 Trafalgar Street – now home accessories shop One In The House

PRINCE GEORGE, 5 Trafalgar Street – now *The George* vegetarian pub

PRINCE ALBERT, 48 Trafalgar Street /Trafalgar House 49 Trafalgar Street – Hertz

STAR OF BRIGHTON,12 Trafalgar Street– Plumbwell Bathrooms

LORD NELSON INN, 36 Trafalgar Street – still public house

HARMONIC TAVERN, 44 Trafalgar Street – Trafalgar Bookshop

SUSSEX YEOMAN, 55 Trafalgar Street/*Battle of Trafalgar*, 61 Trafalgar Street – demolished, now Trafalgar Place

BEE HIVE TAVERN, 85 Trafalgar Street – now new housing

MAID OF THE MILL, 103 – now the *Great Eastern* pub

NORTH ROAD

CHICHESTER ARMS, 98 North Road – now derelict

DOLPHIN, 66-67 North Road, 1858-1970s – now retail premises

RED LION, 99 North Road – now the Foam Shop

Other pubs included the *Moulders Arms* (44), *Norfolk Castle* (54), *Blue Post* (58), *Noah's Ark* (93), *North Road Inn* (102) and the *Golden Cross* (103)

GLOUCESTER ROAD

CANTEEN, 115 Gloucester Road
– private housing
CHARLEVILLE ARMS, 24
Gloucester Road – now Ju Ju
NIGHTINGALE, 96 Gloucester
Road – now Yashar Bish
SHERWOOD FOREST, 17
Gloucester Road – private house
UNION, 28 Gloucester Road –
now Decorative Arts shops

From jar-jar to Ju Ju, Gloucester Road, 2005

WICK INN (formerly Kilham Arms), 41 Gloucester Road – private house

REST OF NORTH LAINE

ABINGDON ARMS, 21 Sydney Street – now Brighton Bead Shop
ST GEORGE AND DRAGON, 32 Sydney Street – now Minky clothing shop
SQUARE AND COMPASS, 18 Over Street – private house
UNITED BROTHERS, 36 Frederick Street – private house
WHEATSHEAF INN, 27 Bond Street – now Velvet gift/interiors shop
BLUE ANCHOR, 29 Kemp Street – private house
CAMDEN ARMS, 34 Kemp Street – private housing, but with shop signs, 'E
Newman' and 'Frigorifico Argentino' (meat stores), dating back to 1914
GAS FITTERS'/BRAZEN STAR, 33 Tidy Street – private house
RISING SUN, 23 Tidy Street – private house
CORPORATION TAVERN, 4 Gardner Street – now Hell's Kitchen
THE HARP, 18 Gardner Street – now Botanica
SUSSEX ARMS, 12 Gardner Street – now Vegetarian Shoes

AROUND TOWN

CITY OF HEREFORD, 29 Upper St James Street – the pub was compulsorily
purchased in 1970 to make way for new flats, and served its last pint on 11
August 1971. Ironically, it had been nominated as one of the top 40 pubs in
Sussex in a Watney's competition. It stood where there is now just an area of
grass next to the flats.

COUNTY OAK, corner of
Carden Hill and County Oak
Avenue – this pub, consisting
of two adjacent V-roofed pre-
fabs, was opened by
Whitbread in September
1950, to serve as the
'Hollingbury housing estate's
very own local'. Its name came
from the oak tree at Crawley
that marked the boundary
between Sussex and Surrey.
The pub – only ever meant as a

The Horse Shoe, Wentworth Street, c1920

temporary establishment – became Hollingbury Library in April 1962 and a new
County Oak was opened the same year.

GOLDEN CROSS, 175 Western Road/corner Marlborough Street – now Top
Shop/Top Man.

HORSE & GROOM, 61a St James Street – now St Mary's Church House.

HORSE SHOE, 10 Wentworth Street – private house, once rented by the famous
writer and broadcaster (and ex-Roedean pupil) Nancy Spain in 1957, so she could
work on a novel called *O Rose*. Instead, she spent more time with her friends,
including Alan Melville and Gilbert Harding, in Brighton's gay pubs. The book was
never finished.

REGENT TAVERN, 3 Church Street – now Dockerill's; no pints, but everything
else, bar the kitchen sink.

UNICORN INN, junction of Queen's Road and North Street – this pub was
demolished in March 1892 (along with the Saracen's Head) to make way for a
new Smithers pub, which in turn was demolished in 1919 and replaced by the
Regent Picture Theatre. It was here that the young John and Roy Boulting, two of
the most important figures in British cinema and creators of the great *Brighton
Rock*, saw their first film. Of course, many films have been seen here since then –
processed in Boot's labs!

CHAPTER TEN

Last Orders?
Pubs in Post-War Brighton

Consigned to history: The City of Hereford (right), Upper St James Street, 1971

During World War II, pubs in Brighton, as they had all over England, played a vital role in community life. But peacetime signalled the start of a decline in many pubs' fortunes, as they struggled to compete with leisure activities, such as television, cinema and restaurants, and urban regeneration.

As the war drew to a close, at least one Brighton pub that had not survived was put to some use: in February 1945, Captain William Ricketts, a veteran of both world wars, and his family – including his own four children, aged 1 to 13, and his sister-in-law and her three children – moved into the disused *Railway Arms* in Freshfield Road. Captain Ricketts was invalided out of the Army in 1944 after serving for four and a half years and subsequently turned out of his rented accommodation in Surrenden Crescent. He said: '*I have searched everywhere for a house but no-one will let to me because of the children*'.

The Brighton Corporation Land and Works Committee suggested that Ricketts and his family move into the *Railway Arms*, which was only furnished with a few camp beds and blankets. An electric cooker was eventually installed by the Corporation.

Post-war development in Brighton, especially around Churchill Square, saw entire streets, including Upper and Little Russell Street, and pubs,

The Sea House, Middle Street, 1987

such as the *Boatman's Arms*, the *Cannon Inn*, *The Flowing Tide* and the *Fisherman At Home*, disappear off the map. One of Brighton's oldest coaching taverns, *The Castle*, was demolished in 1948, the *Eight Bells* in West Street closed by Tamplins in 1964 and even the *Great Globe*, which had seen off smugglers and German warplanes alike, was torn down in February 1965 (although the building that was its sibling, *The Little Globe*, still stands at 153 Edward Street). The *City of Hereford* was compulsory-purchased and demolished in 1971 to make way for new flats in Upper St James Street. The popular *Wheatsheaf Inn* at 27 Bond Street, was the nearest pub to the Theatre Royal's stage. It boasted a passageway that ran from New Road to the back bar where the Prince Regent would entertain Mrs Fitzherbert in private, and also closed in 1971.

As a spokesman for the Licensing Authorities observed in 1965, '*As short a while ago as 1958, you could use a different pub each day of the year without leaving the boundaries of Brighton*'. However, as a Tamplins representative said, '*We have got to move with the times. Some of the older pubs never did do much business and never will. Often the land on which they stand is more valuable than the pubs themselves*'.

In 1970, Watneys closed eight Victorian pubs, including the *Flying Dutchman*. Other much-loved pubs that called '*last orders*' for the final time during the 1970s and 80s were the *Golden Cross* and the *Sea House*.

Adaptation was the key to survival for pubs. Many changed their image, becoming gastro pubs, music pubs, 'family' pubs or themed pubs – aided by more flexible licensing hours, introduced by the Licensing Act of 1988. This permitted alcohol to be sold from 11am to 11pm and 'drinking-up' time extended to 20 minutes; further legislation in 1994 allowed them to open on Sunday afternoons. Cricketers' veteran landlady Winnie Sexton told the Argus, 'At last it means you won't feel like a criminal for standing on licensed property ten minutes after time'.

By the 1980s, nearly 90 per cent of pubs were tied to a brewery, at which point the Conservative government, with its commitment to 'free enterprise', introduced Lord Young's Beer Orders, which forced the big breweries to sell off thousands of tied pubs. The Monopolies and Mergers Commission set a October 1992 deadline for the breweries to sell off many of their pubs. Some companies, such as Inntrepeneur, part of the Grand Metropolitan empire in 1991, imposed rent rises on tenants to offset 'losses' as pubs now allowed to sell guest beers from rival brewers, and tenants were told they had to sign 20-year leases – or quit. By 1991, 20 per cent of Brighton's then 280 pubs were up for sale.

This industry deregulation, in turn, spawned a new breed of 'pubcos', such as Enterprise Inns and Punch Taverns which together, by 2004, owned more than a quarter of Britain's pubs. It also prompted the rise of the Hobgoblin, Hogshead and Firkin chains – anathema to pub traditionalists. In 1998, Howard Trevette, manager of the Pool Valley bus station, warned, 'We are becoming the swill bin of the South. The police will have trouble coping with all these new places'. The Brighton Licensed Victuallers' Association demanded a meeting with the council over their concerns about pubco domination.
Like the big breweries before them, some of the pubcos have come under criticism from their own tenants, who have claimed that unfair rent rises have pushed up beer prices. A subsequent Trade & Industry Select Committee investigation into the pubcos' dominance and practises found that no one company or brewer held a dominant position, but rather fudged the 'beer tie' issue.

Now, Brighton's pubs face a slew of new challenges from laws. The Disability Discrimination Act (DDA) decreed that by October 1 2004, pubs had to ensure that they were accessible to the UK's 8.5 million people with disabilities, including adapting the buildings – and staff attitudes. However, a survey carried out by The Publican before the law came into effect showed that 48 per cent of respondent licensees said they had done nothing to comply with the DDA. Whether it's down to complacency, apathy or stubbornness, the attitude of these publicans makes no sense – at the very least, in commercial terms: according to Peter Kemp, chairman of the National Forum of Wheelchair User Group, *'Disabled people across the United Kingdom have a combined spending power of £54bn per year'*.

From 7 February, Brighton's council took over responsibility for licensing from magistrates and implementing new licensing legislation in the city's pubs and bars. The four main licensing objectives are prevention of crime and disorder; public safety; prevention of public nuisance and protection of children from harm; increasing pressure on publicans to play their part in reducing drink-fuelled anti-social behaviour. There will now be four types of licence – Premises Licences, Personal Licences, Temporary Event Notices and Club Premises Certificates. Subject to council approval, licensees will be able to choose the days and times they wish to sell alcohol or provide entertainment, and flexible opening hours, subject to the consideration of the impact on residents. Prospective licensees will be checked for suitability and a criminal record.

Brighton & Hove Council say their aim is *'to produce a balanced package providing flexibility and safeguards which is simple transparent and accountable'*, able to:
- clamp down on the crime, disorder and anti-social behaviour perpetrated by a minority, whilst giving the responsible majority more freedom and choice about how they spend their leisure time
- to encourage tourism
- to give the public a greater say in the licensing process
- to encourage a more civilised and responsible approach to alcohol consumption
- to reduce the burden of unnecessary regulation on business.

The final handover from magistrates to local authorities is scheduled to take place in November 2005.

In its 2004 Industry Report, *The Publican* revealed that the new licensing laws were overwhelmingly the biggest concern for publicans. However, this report was published before the announcement of the government's 2005 White Paper on Public Health, which proposed banning smoking from pubs that serve food. Only private clubs, where members voted to allow smoking, and pubs which do not serve prepared food, would be exempt. In other words, pubs that serve food prepared on the premises or in *'unwrapped' form, will not escape the ban'*; smoking may be allowed if the pub serves, for example, sandwiches in sealed packets and packets of crisps.

With the unusually high number of Brighton pubs that make a feature of their 'home cooked food', the implications are enormous.

In response to the White Paper, Mark Hastings, of the British Beer and Pubs Association, said that within four years, 80 per cent of pub space would be non-smoking: *'At lunchtime far more of a pub is changed into an eating area than it is in the evenings. How does that work if you have a ban on smoking in all areas where food is served? Does it cover bar snacks?'*. The BBPA's most pessimistic estimates claim that a quarter of all pubs would drop their food menus in order to keep their smoking customers, and up to 75,000 jobs and hundreds of pubs could be lost if an outright ban is introduced. Of course, these losses have to be weighed up against the 114,000 lives lost in Britain each year from tobacco use, according to ASH (Action on Smoking & Health UK).

Under the current plans – on which Health Secretary John Reid promised wide public and industry consulation – smoking restrictions will be phased in, with a ban on smoking in NHS and government buildings by 2006; enclosed public places by 2007 and licensed premises by the end of 2008.

Amongst those who welcome the proposals were Ed Gershon, of pubco JD Wetherspoon, who thought *'It will bring a lot more people back into pubs long-term'*. This was followed by the announcement in January 2005 that the chain would ban smoking in all its 650 venues by May 2006; 60 would become smoke-free zones from May 2005. Five other major pubcos – Enterprise Inns, Mitchells & Butlers, Punch Taverns, Scottish & Newcastle and Spirit Group – which own 22,000 outlets between them, had also already agreed a no-smoking initiative in September 2004 which stated that by the end of 2005, all their premises would have:

- No smoking at the bar
- No smoking in back-of-house areas
- Reduced floor space area for customers who smoke, to a maximum 20 per cent by December 2009
- A minimum of 50 per cent of dining areas to be non-smoking

Brighton & Hove's Big Smoke Debate involved a survey carried out for the city's NHS Primary Care Trust – 83 per cent of the 3,700 respondents favoured a ban on smoking in public spaces. In December 2004, John Woodruff, landlord of the Swan at Falmer, became the first publican in the Brighton area to voluntarily impose a smoking ban in his premises. Mr Woodruff said, *'I haven't noticed a drop in profits. There have been people who said they came because we were a non-smoking pub'*.

From February 7 2005, new legislation allowed all licensed premises to open around the clock. However, canvassed members of the BBPA said they would be happy with opening for just an extra hour or two a day, at weekends only. This contradicted the government's own research, which estimated that more than 35,000 pubs would seek to extend their licenses to open until about 2am. The BBPA's Mark Hastings claimed that 'There is not a single pub in the country that intends to open for 24 hours', while a survey carried out by Brighton magazine *The*

24 hour drinking? Ha ha… Ha Ha Bar, Pavilion Buildings, 2005

Insight revealed that 65 per cent of its readers favoured 24-hour opening. The legislation was opposed by a 'rainbow' coalition of voices: Mark Jones, CEO of the Yates Group, owners of Brighton's *Ha Ha Bar*, said he was *'totally opposed to the change in the law…this is coming at the wrong time for the industry. We are under huge pressure over binge drinking'*. Alcohol Concern said, *'Given the UK's prevailing drinking culture, these changes are more likely to increase crime and disorder rather than curb it'*.

Other dissenters included the Tories (who, in 1988, introduced all-day drinking), the Liberal Democrats, a good number of rebel Labour MPs and outgoing Metropolitan police chief, Sir John Stevens, fearing, like Mark Jones, that it would fuel an increase in anti-social behaviour and 'binge' drinking.

The costs of this latter-day social ill are well-known to health service workers locally and nationally. The Office for National Statistics published figures in February 2005 revealed that the number of people dying from alcohol-related illnesses, including liver disease, is rising. A report in September 2004 said that binge-drinking culture cost NHS 1.7bn a year, with 1.2 million incidents a year of alcohol-related violence. These figures were backed up by the testimony of Dr Paul Ransom, at the casualty department at the Royal Sussex hospital, which revealed the 'price of a pint': *'Almost every assault is alcohol related, especially during the weekend. Alcohol is a lubricator for all sorts of things. To put it crudely, in men it fuels fights and in women it fuels overdoses after a row. We could get by with a quarter of the staff on the evening shifts if it wasn't for alcohol. I would like to see money available to fund an alcohol worker on our A&E...I think the people who should pay for it are the breweries, not the government or social services.'* It also emerged that between 60 and 80 per cent of people kept in the hospital's observations wards overnight were there because of alcoholic over-indulgence.

Many pubs in Brighton – as elsewhere – are increasingly aiming at attracting the under-30s, particularly the 18-25 age group, and this presents a new generation of problems. A 2004 British Medical Journal report found that the number of teenage girls taken to hospital with mental and behavioural problems caused by alcohol had risen sharply, by 24 per cent in under-14s and 9 per cent in the 15-24 age group. This goes hand-in-hand with a 2005 study of teenage drinking across Europe, which revealed that girls were now bigger binge-drinkers than boys.
However, some statistics contradict these findings: a national survey on teenage lifestyles in 2004 showed that the current generation of teenagers were spending less on alcohol than ever, choosing to use it to buy fast food, clothes, films and music, and mobile phones. Interestingly, the survey was carried out by Ukclubculture, an organisation that hosts 400 alcohol-free clubbing events a year for under-18s.

In recent years, it has been officially recognised that the pub is an integral part of British life: in December 2004, the Home Office published a 25-page handbook for immigrants which gave them a potted history of the UK, providing information on everything from how to open a bank account to what a traditional Christmas entails. The booklet also contained information about pubs, including how to get served at the bar, as well as the sound advice that *'If you spill a stranger's drink by accident, it is good manners (and prudent) to offer to buy another'.*

In 1996, the Brewers and Licensed Retailers' Assocation published Kate Fox's comprehensive *Passport To The Pub: The Tourist's Guide To Pub Etiquette*, which has been republished several times since. It sets its store in its opening sentences, telling visitors *'By all means visit Stonehenge and Buckingham Palace, but if you want to see what real life in Britain is all about, you have to go to the pub'*.

The rumoured death of the British pub – and Brighton's pubs in particular – has, Mark Twain-like, often been announced, predicted and exaggerated. The pessimists predict that their demise will be hastened by a combination of the new legislation and other factors, including the increasing numbers of people switching from having a pint in their local to sharing a bottle of wine at home or over a restaurant meal, and the proliferation of bland, soulless chain pubs.

However, other Brighton publicans have taken a different, more optimistic approach to these social and legal developments. As has been the case for over 150 years, these can bring changes in their wake that can be weathered. The best example is to be found in the Golden Lion group's Brighton pubs, which includes the Cricketers, the Colonnade and the Marine Tavern, which have kept their customers' loyalty by placing the emphasis on 'real', 'traditional' and 'local'. Perhaps it was Brenda Elsip, landlady of The Temple bar, who expressed the most realistic overview of the current state of Brighton's boozers when she said, *'Brighton's big enough and diverse enough to have a variety of outlets. I think there's a place for all of us'.*
Long may it continue to be so.
Cheers!

Name Above the Door: How Some Pubs Got Their Names

BAT AND BALL, 51 Ditchling Road.
The name came from The Level, which was used for cricket matches until the 1820s.

CONSTANT SERVICE, Islingword Road.
Named after the Constant Service Water Company who owned the building in 1853 when it was a pumping station.

COUNTY OAK, corner of Carden Hill and County Oak Avenue.
The name came from the oak tree at Crawley marking boundary between Sussex and Surrey.

c1987

CRICKETERS, 15 Black Lion Street.
What is generally regarded as Brighton's oldest pub started life as the Laste & Fishcart (a laste being a measure of fish) as the old fish market was nearby. In 1790, Thomas Jutton, a famous local cricketer, bought and renamed it.

DOG TRAY, 10 Edward Street
'Tray' was a popular name for dogs in the Victorian era and this pub began as the Old Dog Tray in 1870. The name also featured in Heinrich Hoffman's poem 'Cruel Frederick' in the 1844 German children's book Struwwelpeter: *'The good Dog Tray is happy now, he has no time to say bow-wow'.*

1984

c1911

FREE BUTT, Albion Street.
Built in 1821, this was originally part of the Phoenix Brewery. Its name may have come from the Army shooting range (butt) nearby, but another story tells that the landlord would sometimes give lucky customers a free butt of ale!

GEESE HAVE GONE OVER THE WATER, Southover Street.
Originally The Golden Cross, Irish landlord Cyril Bourke took over the pub in May 1988 and gave it its new name, which refers to the period in sixteenth century Irish history when the nobility, artists and poets of Ireland fled to escape English rule, also known as the "Flight of the Earls".

GOOD COMPANIONS, 132 Dyke Road.
Formerly Chichester Lodge, a private house, this pub was opened in 1939, the day after World War II was declared. It was named after a famous railway engine and, appropriately, the Brighton station master used to be a regular punter.

1986

1987

HOLE IN THE WALL, formerly Queensbury Arms, 12 Queensbury Mews.
Said to be Brighton's smallest pub, it was named after the infamous Marquess of Queensberry [sic], father of Lord Alfred Douglas and scourge of Oscar Wilde, who owned a seafront house for many years. Its current name comes from the days when Royal Fusiliers stationed nearby would be served their drinks through a hole in the wall.

LONDON UNITY, Islingword Road.
Opened as an alehouse in 1872, this pub is named after the packet ship which, in 1821, rescued a balloonist who had taken off from Black Rock to fly to France, but came down in the Channel.

1987

MAZEPPA INN, 19 Ann Street:.
Now the site of St Bartholomews School, the pub was bought by Brighton Corporation from A H Steel in 1967. Hetman Ivan Mazeppa was an 18th century Cossack Ukranian separatist, who inspired poems by Pushkin and Byron and an opera by Tchaikovsky.

1969

c1932

OBED ARMS, 126 Albion Hill, on corner of Dinapore Street. This pub, built in 1860, and the street name had their origins in India – Dinapore being the name of a town involved in the Indian mutiny of 1857.

PECHELL ARMS, 17/18 Market Street.
Admiral Sir George Pechell was the MP for Brighton from 1836 to1860.

PEDESTRIAN ARMS, 13 Foundry Street:
Opened in 1858 as *The White Horse*, it became the *Labour in Vain* in 1862, then, briefly, *The Lamb*. It gained its current name in 1869 when taken over by John Stepney, champion long-distance roadwalker and competitor in many London to Brighton walks.

1976

c1990

PUMP HOUSE, 46 Market Street: Dating back to 1776, its name comes from the pump house that fed sea water to William's Baths.

Brighton's Theme Pubs

PLACE NAMES

Abergavenny Arms; Abyssinia Arms; City of Brunswick/Hereford/York/London. Crystal Palace Tavern; Denmark Tavern; Derby Arms; Devonshire Arms; Dorset Arms; Dover Castle; Exmouth Tavern; Italian Arms; Liverpool Arms; Lewes Castle; Norfolk Arms; Northumberland; Quebec; Sherwood Forest.

ROYALTY

Balmoral; Crown; Duke of Baden; Duke of Cambridge; Duke of Connaught; Duke of Edinburgh; Duke of Wellington; George IV; King and Queen; Lord Clyde; Prince Albert/Alfred/Arthur; George; Princess Helena; Prince of Wales; Princess Victoria; Queen's Arms/Head/Tavern/Park; Regency; Royal Albert; Royal George; Royal Princess; Royal Sovereign; Royal Standard; Three Kings; Victoria; William IV.

NAUTICAL

Anchor; Blue Anchor; Little Yacht; Lord Nelson; Admiral Napier; Marine Tavern; Neptune Inn; New Pier Tavern; Ocean Wave; Pier Tavern; Pilot; Schooner; Sea House; Sea Serpent; Ship; South Coast Tavern; Victory; Yacht and Anchor.

MILITARY

Artillery Arms; Balaclava Tavern; Battle of Trafalgar; Battle of Waterloo; Bugle; Admiral Napier; Cannon; Conqueror; Flying Scud; Fortune of War; Gun Inn; Helmet; Hero of Waterloo; Napoleon III; Rifleman; Royal Dragoon; Royal Hussar; Royal Standard; Volunteer; Wellington; Volunteer; Sussex Yeoman.

NATURE

Comet; Dolphin; Eclipse; Evening Star (one of the rarest pub names); Flowing Tide; Flowing Stream; Full Moon; Half Moon; Merry Harriers; Morning Star; Nightingale Tavern; Noah's Ark (93 North Road); Old Hoss; Orange Tree; Rising Sun; Seven Stars; Stag; Phoenix; Star; Star in the East; Star of Bedford; Star of Brunswick ; Swan; Three Elms; Unicorn; Western Star; White Eagle; Eagle; White Hart; White Horse; Black Horse.

TRADES

Artilleryman; Basketmakers' ; Blacksmiths; Boatman; Brassfounder's; Brewers; Bricklayers; British Rifleman; Cabinet Makers'; Carpenters; Coachmakers; Cricketers; Dragoon; Farriers'; Fire Brigade Arms; Fisherman at Home; Fitters; Fishmongers; Flyman's Home; Forester & Shepherd; Gardeners; Gasfitters; Joiners; Laundry Tavern; Locksmiths; Locomotive Inn; Maltsters'; Market Inn; Mason's; Mechanics; Millers; Moulders; Painters; Plasterers; Railway Guard; Sawyers; Three Jolly Butchers; Wheelwrights; Woodman.

INDEX

Abbey, Henry, 11
Abbey, William, 11
Abinger House, 54
Albany Tavern, 32
Albermarle, 35, 58
Amber Ale, 11
Ancient Order of Froth Blowers, 33
Appleton Alfred, 32
Aquarium Inn, 39, 58
Ashworth, Ellen 'Bubbles', 32
ASH (Action on Smoking & Health UK), 70
Australian Walkabout, 23
Barmaids' Political Defence League, 43
Barnard, Mary, 1
Barnard Sarah, 1
Bat & Ball, 25, 74
Bath Arms, 22, 54
Battle of Waterloo, 23
The Bedford Tavern, 24
Beer Shop Act 1830, 2, 53
Belvedere, 35
Bennett, Peter, 5
Black Horse, 39
Black Lion, 1
Black Lion Brewery, 8
The Blew Inn, 2
Block House, 50
Brewers (Brighton), 8-14
Brewers and Licensed Retailers' Assocation, 73
Brewers' Society, 40
British Beer and Pubs Association, 58, 70, 71
Brighton & Hove's Big Smoke Debate, 70
Brighton Lesbian Group, 37
Brighton Licensing Project, 20
Brighton Licensed Victuallers' Association, 50, 68
Brighton Society for the Prosecution of Thieves, 19
Brown Sheila, 5
Bugle Inn, 22
Bulldog, 36
Burtenshaw Colin, 50
Burtenshaw Sarah, 27
Burtenshaw Thomas, 27
Burton Peter, 36, 37
Cadets of Temperance, 42
Canadian soldiers, 19-20
Canterbury Hall, 53
Carver Deryck, 8
Castle, 1, 2, 15, 67
The Caves, 38
Caxton Arms, 37
Chapman William, 8
City of Hereford, 50, 64, 67
City of York, 56
Coach and Horses, 15, 52, 53
Cokelers, 42
Collins, Captain Fred, 27-29
Collins Fred Junior, 28
Colonnade, 30, 31
Constant Service, 31
County Oak, 65, 74
Cowley Harry, 31
Cranbourne Arms, 58
Crane Thomas, 42
Cricketers, 16, 22, 29, 37, 56, 68, 74
Crown, 2, 52
C-Side, 5, 6
Dark Star, 14
Defence of the Realm Act (DORA), 3, 44

Disability Discrimination Act (DDA), 68-69

Dog Tray, 74

D'Onston Roslyn, 16

Dorset Arms, 37

Druid's Head, 2, 15, 22

Eagle, 23, 61

Earth and Stars, 5

Edlin Emily, 25, 27

Edlin Tubby, 27

Elwes 'Blind Harry', 32

Farr Tommy, 18

Flowing Tide, 19

Fortune of War, 6, 35

Free Butt, 31, 75

Fuller John, 17

Full Moon, 57, 59

Fury Ray, 30

Geese Have Gone Over The Water, 75

George, 23, 31, 61

George Beard, 23

George Gavin, 5

Glass excise duty, 3

Gloucester, 6, 54

Golden Fleece, 35

Golden Cross, 65

Good Companions, 75

Good Intent, 18

Gore-Booth Eva, 43

Great Eastern, 61

Great Globe, 4, 15

Green Dragon, 18, 19

Greyhound, 35

Griffith, George, 12

Ha Ha Bar, 22, 71

Hallett, William, 10

Hanbury Arms, 4, 25, 37, 55

Hand In Hand, 14

Harding Gilbert, 31

Harlequin, 22, 39

Harton Harriet, 17

Hazelgrove Edith and Henry, 29

Heart In Hand, 37

Henekey's New Ship Inn, 16

Hervey Arms, 20

Hilton, Daisy and Violet, 26-27

Hilton Mary, 26

Holloway Lily, 29

Hole in the Wall, 75

Horse & Groom, 65

Horse Shoe, 65

Huggett PC, 17

Hunter Horace, 30

Hutchinson Captain, 4, 47

Iron Duke, 37

Jolly Fisherman, 17

Jury's Out, 39

Kensington, 57

King and Queen, 17, 52, 55, 57, 58

King's Arms, 3, 15

Kruger Beer Company, 3

Lawrence John, 18

Leigh John, 17

Lewes Road Inn, 23

Licensing Act 1872, 3, 42

Licensing Act 1988, 68

Lion and Lobster, 60

Lion and Unicorn, 18

Little Globe, 67

Lloyd George David, 44

London Unity, 75

Longhurst, Henry, 11

MacDonald Margaret, 43

Marchant William, 52

Markwell's Bar, 36

Marlborough, 5, 36, 56

Martha Gunn's, 57

Martin Albert, 30

Mash Tun, 5, 25
Maugham, Robin, 31
Mazeppa Inn, 76
Metcalfe Henry, 23
Monopolies and Mergers Commission, 68
Montgomery John, 35
Montpelier Inn, 57
Morton-George Mike, 59
National Freedom Defence League, 44
National Union of Women Workers' Joint Committee on the Employment of Barmaids, 43
New Heart in Hand, 37
New Pier Tavern, 32, 35
Nicholls Albert, 4
Norfolk LA, 49
No Treating Order, 45
Obed Arms, 76
O'Donnell James, 18
Old Strike A Light, 21
Open House, 54
Oriental, 37
Overall Mrs, 32
Packham Lucy, 18, 23
Packham Tom, 18
Park View, 24
Pechell Arms, 76
Pedestrian Arms, 29, 76
Penfold Jackie, 18
People's Pubs, 6
Pickwick Bar, 58
Pigott's, 34
PSA (Pleasant Sunday Afternoon) Temperance Committee, 45
Pond, 32
Prestonville Arms, 22
Prince Albert, 59, 60
Princess Victoria, 37

Prostitution, 16
Pump House, 22, 60, 76
Punch Taverns, 68
Quadrant, 36
Queen's Arms, 39
Queen's Head, 39
Railway Arms, 66-67
Ransom Dr Paul, 72
Ranson Det Chief Roy, 36
Regency Tavern, 2, 18, 24, 37, 56
Regent Tavern, 65
Riches Norman, 38
Richmond, 57
Ricketts Captain William, 66
Rising Sun, 21
Robin Hood, 6
Robbins, Bev and Brenda, 14
Rock, 23
Rockingham Inn, 38
Rowntree Joseph, 40
Royal Commission on Licensing 1931, 20
Royal Pavilion Tavern, 22, 59
Ruffer Ernest, 32
Running Horse, 19
St James Tavern, 34, 36
Sassoon family mausoleum, 25
Scannell Eddie, 30
Sea House, 15, 59, 67
Seven Stars, 1, 55
Sexton Winnie, 29, 37
Sherrott Councillor Joseph, 3
Shoosmith WH, 42
Sims, George, 40
Smithers Henry, 8
Smithers Edward, 8
Snowden, Viscount, 41
Soar David 'Mad Dog', 18
Sons of Temperance, 41

Spencer Colin, 34, 35

Spotted Dog, 1, 35, 38

Squid and Starfish, 6

Stag Inn, 22

Stamford Arms, 36

Star & Garter, 2, 24, 52

Sudeley Arms, 60

Sussex GLF, 36

Sussex Arms, 22, 31

Swan (Falmer), 70

Tamplin, Richard, 12

Teeling William, 34

Thatched House, 54

Thomas Maria, 45

Three Jolly Butchers, 35

Thurlow Arms, 35

Ukclubculture, 72

Unicorn, 1, 65

Vallance and Son, 8

Vallance & Catt, 8

Vasso, 58

Volunteer, 58

Vulcan, 41

Waggon & Horses, 31, 32

Watney Mann, 13, 67

Welcome Brothers, 27, 28

JD Wetherspoon, 70

Wheatsheaf, 67

Whitehawk Inn, 60

White Horse, 52

White Lion, 19

William IV, 30

Winder, George, 28

Zelgrain, 5, 59